Pentacles

ARCANA LIBRARY

Volume One

Pentacles

A Theology of Matter and the Authority of What Endures

Kristi Hall

GRIST THEOLOGY

This book was written with the assistance of AI tools. The theological argument, the structural decisions, and the voice are the author's own, developed over years of study and practice. AI was used as a collaborator for drafting illustrative examples, tightening prose, and thinking through specific structural problems. Every word in these pages has been chosen and accepted by the author, who takes full responsibility for the contents.

ISBN: 979-8-9949106-7-2

First edition, 2026

Published by Grist Theology — gristtheology.com

Also by Kristi Hall

Imbolc: A Theology of Winter and the Making of Spring

The Timing Wound: Sacred Return and the End of Perpetual Offering

Beltane: A Theology of Fire and the Proof of Form

DEDICATION

This is the Tarot program I always wanted. The cards have been my tireless companions for decades — seeing me through all the joys and difficulties of life. They always tell the truth, if we will only listen.

Authority does not belong to what shines brightest or moves fastest — it belongs to what lasts.

CONTENTS

How This Book Is Built

Each card in the Arcana Library is approached through five layers — five different ways of meeting the same card.

Foundation names what the card governs — the structural condition it describes.

Imagery reads the Rider–Waite–Smith image directly: figure, posture, environment, object, absence.

Tradition places the card within the historical and mythic ground from which its imagery emerged.

Meditation is delivered as recorded audio. Each card has its own. They are available at gristtheology.com/arcana.

Journaling lives in the companion workbook, which carries the diagnostic and contemplative work the layers above are designed to make possible.

This volume contains the first three layers. They carry the theology of each card — what it is, what it depicts, where it came from. A reader with only this book has the doctrine in full.

The remaining two layers carry the experience. The recorded meditations let each card be entered rather than read about; the workbook prompts let it be worked through in your own life. They are designed to run alongside the reading, card by card, so the doctrine can be inhabited and not only understood.

OPENING

Prelude

The Arcana as Law, Not Language

The Arcana Library approaches Tarot differently than most modern treatments. Here, the cards are not treated as a symbolic language to be decoded – they are approached as structures to be recognized. The system functions less like a language and more like a map. What follows establishes the orientation that shapes everything else.

What Is Meant by "Law"

When this book uses the word law, it is not referring to rules, commands, or obligations. It refers to structure. A law, in this sense, describes how something tends to behave under certain conditions. Gravity is a law. Seasons follow laws. Bodies change according to laws. None of these require belief or obedience. They simply describe what happens when we move within them.

The Arcana operate in much the same way. They do not instruct or demand. They describe patterns that tend to unfold. You retain agency at all times. You may move with a structure, resist it, ignore it, or work against it. The Tarot does not judge these choices. It helps clarify their effects.

Here, law is a form of orientation – not enforcement.

Tarot as Inherited Structure, Not Personal Oracle

The Tarot did not originate as a personal oracle meant to answer individual questions. It emerged from a symbolic worldview in which images carried shared knowledge about survival, authority, loss, transformation, and continuity. Its figures function more like roles than personalities. Its sequences describe conditions rather than stories. When Tarot is treated solely as a personal oracle, meaning becomes highly flexible – shaped by mood, preference, or desire. While this can feel intimate and empowering, it can also loosen the Tarot's grounding presence. The Arcana Library begins from that grounding. Here, the cards are approached as structures that can be recognized over time, rather than messages that must be decoded in the moment. Meaning is not something you are asked to invent. It arises through relationship and return.

Why Meaning Is Received, Not Invented

In a structural system, meaning doesn't arrive all at once. It gathers through contact. Just as a landscape becomes familiar through repeated passage rather than explanation, the Tarot reveals itself through sustained engagement. The cards remain consistent even as personal circumstances change. That consistency is not a limitation – it's what makes the system trustworthy.

Receiving meaning does not mean surrendering interpretation. It means allowing the structure to exist independently of preference before responding to it. This posture slows the urge to explain and opens space for recognition.

The Place of Intuition

Intuition is not dismissed in this book – it is simply repositioned. When intuition operates without structure, it often mirrors existing beliefs or emotional states. Structure brings a gentle kind of friction. You might sit with the Ten of Pentacles, for instance, and feel an immediate pull toward themes of wealth or family legacy – but the structure asks you to stay longer, to notice that the card is also about what happens when continuity no longer requires effort. That pause between first impression and deeper recognition is where the friction lives.

By encountering symbols that don't immediately conform to expectation, intuition becomes more responsive and less self-referential. The Tarot doesn't replace intuition. It gives intuition something steady to meet.

Why Myth Comes First

Many modern Tarot approaches begin with psychology: cards as inner states, archetypes as aspects of the self, spreads as mirrors of personal process. This book begins one step earlier. Myth is not metaphor. It is a way of organizing reality before it becomes personal. Psychology helps describe how individuals experience these patterns internally. Myth describes the patterns themselves. By starting with mythic and symbolic structure, the book allows psychological insight – when it arises – to rest on something shared and stable, rather than subjective.

Psychology explains experience. Myth explains why experience takes the shape it does.

The Source of the Imagery

One further orientation belongs here, before the cards begin.

The Rider–Waite–Smith deck is not culturally neutral. Its imagery is drawn from medieval and early modern Europe – manorial fields, walled towns, almsgiving outside cathedral doors, guild workshops, knights and stewards, the iconography of the Christian liturgical year. The Pentacles suit in particular preserves the social world of agrarian Europe with unusual specificity.

This book honors that specificity rather than disguising it. When the Tradition layer describes the demesne, the entail, the reeve and bailiff, the apprentice's bench, or the alms before the cathedral, it is reading what the imagery actually depicts – not importing those references for atmosphere. The cards' historical ground is European-Christianfeudal in origin, and the structural patterns the cards encode were shaped within that world.

Naming this is not the same as endorsing it. The book draws on these historical structures because they are what the imagery records, and because the patterns they preserve – provision, holding, exposure, redistribution, repetition, sufficiency, inheritance – describe conditions that recur far beyond their original setting. Other traditions encode similar patterns in different forms. This book reads one tradition closely. It does not claim that tradition is the only one that matters, or the one that should govern others.

What follows takes the imagery seriously by reading it as it is.

A Closing Orientation

Nothing here asks you to abandon the way you already work with Tarot. It asks you to set it aside for a time. What follows works structurally – by recognition rather than interpretation – and recognition forms through repeated contact, not through effort. The Tarot does not require fluency to function. It requires duration.

Timing, Viability, and Authority

The Tarot is often approached as a way to answer questions about what will happen next. That's an understandable impulse. When something matters to us, we want clarity, direction, and reassurance about where a situation is heading. The Arcana Library invites a slightly different way of listening.

Rather than specializing in outcomes, the Tarot is especially attuned to timing — to when something is able to take shape, when it is still forming, and when its moment has already passed. What follows names a central principle of this work: the cards are often less concerned with events themselves than with the conditions surrounding them. Learning to recognize those conditions doesn't reduce choice — it tends to widen it.

When Rather Than What

Human attention naturally looks for content. We want to know what something means, where it leads, and how it resolves. Tarot is frequently used to meet this need. The Arcana operate at a different level.

Instead of describing specific outcomes, the cards point toward phases of readiness. They indicate when something is viable, when it is still too early, and when its usefulness has already begun to wane. In this sense, they describe when rather than what. This is why the same card can appear in very different situations without losing relevance. The card isn't naming a single event. It's identifying a timing condition — one that can express itself in many forms.

Viability as a Measure of Possibility

Viability refers to whether something can be sustained once it enters form. An idea can be compelling and still be unviable. A relationship can be sincere and still be unsustainable. A truth can be accurate and still cause harm if introduced too soon.

The Tarot doesn't deny these realities. It helps place them in context. By naming viability, the cards help distinguish between what is present in principle and what can actually be carried in practice. This distinction allows movement without urgency and restraint without suppression.

Revelation and Preservation

Modern spiritual culture often treats revelation as an unquestioned good — as though what is true should always be expressed immediately. The Tarot takes a more patient view. Some things need time. Some truths require protection before they can be shared. Some forces need to remain sheltered until the conditions that can support them are in place.

This isn't secrecy for its own sake. It's care.

Consider the High Priestess. She sits between two pillars, a scroll partially concealed in her lap. What she holds is not hidden out of refusal — it is held because the conditions for its full reception are not yet present. She does not deny what she carries. She preserves it until it can be met. This is the difference between withholding and tending.

The Arcana include moments of emergence and moments of holding back. Both are part of continuity. Without preservation, revelation can damage what it brings into view. The Tarot doesn't favor exposure. It favors what can endure.

Authority Without Coercion

In this book, authority doesn't mean instruction or command. It refers to reliability — the way a structure continues to describe conditions accurately over time. The authority of the Tarot lies in its steadiness. Its symbols tend to remain relevant whether or not they are welcomed, believed, or fully understood. This consistency allows the cards to serve as points of orientation rather than directives.

Authority, in this sense, doesn't remove agency. It makes relationship possible.

Cards as Regulators of Emergence

Some Tarot cards mark moments when movement outward is supported. Others indicate times when emergence would place something fragile at risk. These cards don't function as gatekeepers. They don't block action. They describe the conditions under which movement is more likely to be viable — or more likely to cause harm.

Seen this way, the Tarot isn't permissive or prohibitive. It doesn't say yes or no. It describes readiness. Recognizing that readiness doesn't obligate compliance. A person may speak when silence would preserve. Act when waiting would stabilize. Remain when movement would ease pressure. The Tarot doesn't remove these options. What it offers is informed choice. By helping distinguish between presence and readiness, the cards expand the range of possible responses. They don't dictate behavior. They help illuminate consequence. What happens next is still a matter of choice.

A Closing Orientation

The shift this asks for is small. Rather than asking what the Tarot is saying, notice what phase it seems to be naming. Rather than seeking instruction, pay attention to the conditions being described.

Timing is not destiny. Viability is not prohibition. Authority is not control. They are ways of recognizing when something can safely take shape.

Symbolic Reality

People meet the Tarot through many different lenses – cultural, psychological, aesthetic, spiritual – and still the symbols continue to describe familiar conditions. Patterns repeat. Structures persist. The cards remain relevant even when they are approached imperfectly or without full understanding. This can be easy to miss, especially in a culture that places great emphasis on interpretation, accuracy, and personal meaning. And yet it happens consistently enough to deserve attention.

What follows explores why.

Symbols as Living Structures

In the Arcana Library, symbols are not treated as metaphors or poetic stand-ins for inner states. They are approached as living structures – forms that organize experience whether or not they are consciously named. A living structure doesn't depend on explanation to exist. A road remains a road whether or not it is labeled. A threshold still functions as a threshold even when it is crossed without awareness.

Tarot symbols work in much the same way. They describe how forces tend to arrange themselves in lived experience. They remain coherent across time and culture because they reflect patterns that recur regardless of language, belief, or interpretive skill.

Symbolic Reality as Environment

Symbolic reality is often assumed to be abstract or subjective – real only insofar as it is imagined, felt, or believed. This book approaches it more concretely.

Here, symbolic reality is understood as an environment – not a metaphor for one, but a space with actual contours. It is shaped by attention, memory, timing, and repetition. You have likely already felt its texture without naming it: the way a particular card seems to arrive during a particular kind of season in your life. The way certain images carry weight before you can explain why. The way a spread can feel precise even when you can't articulate what it's saying.

These aren't projections. They're contact.

Like physical environments, symbolic reality has limits. Certain movements feel supported. Others bring strain. Some conditions allow continuity, while others make it difficult. The Tarot doesn't create this symbolic environment. It helps you notice where you already are.

Why Tarot Works Without Mastery

Because Tarot symbols describe structure rather than opinion, they don't require mastery to be effective. A person doesn't need to believe in Tarot, understand its history, interpret it "correctly," or feel especially intuitive for the symbols to remain relevant. The cards continue to describe conditions even when understanding is partial or uncertain.

This is why readings often feel accurate even when the language used to describe them is imprecise. The symbol has already oriented attention toward a real condition. Meaning may be incomplete, but contact has occurred. The Tarot is forgiving in this way. It doesn't depend on perfect interpretation to function. Misunderstanding a symbol doesn't make it inert — it may blur clarity or shape how something is expressed, but the underlying structure remains present.

This doesn't make interpretation unimportant. It simply places it later in the relationship. Understanding can deepen contact, but contact exists before understanding. The Tarot doesn't respond to expertise. It responds to engagement over time.

Symbolic Structure and Choice

Recognizing symbolic structure doesn't remove choice. A person may notice a pattern and still choose not to engage it. They may move against timing, resist containment, or ignore maintenance. Symbolic reality doesn't compel alignment. It responds to interaction.

Awareness changes relationship. Relationship shapes outcome. This is the role Tarot plays — not to direct action, but to make conditions visible.

The Stability of Symbolic Reality

Symbolic reality persists because it is grounded in lived experience rather than abstract theory. Human experience follows recognizable patterns over time: beginnings and endings, effort and rest, attachment and release, endurance and change. Tarot symbols endure because they reflect the way these patterns take shape in lived life.

This is why Tarot remains useful even as cultural frameworks change. It doesn't rely on any single belief system. It rests on shared realities of life as it is lived.

A Closing Orientation

With this, the Prelude's theological groundwork is in place. You've encountered Tarot as structure rather than language, timing rather than outcome, and symbolic reality rather than personal projection. Nothing here asks you to change how you already work with Tarot. The intention isn't to replace existing practice, but to widen the field in which Tarot can be understood.

Before we enter the suits, one question remains: why this deck?

Why Rider–Waite–Smith?

Before we enter the suits, it's worth naming a practical choice that shapes this work: the Arcana Library uses the Rider–Waite–Smith deck as its primary visual and symbolic reference. This choice is not about preference, trend, or authority. It is about continuity, clarity, and shared structure.

A Common Symbolic Baseline

The Rider–Waite–Smith deck provides a shared symbolic baseline that many Tarot readers — across traditions, cultures, and decades — already recognize. Its imagery has become the reference point through which much modern Tarot understanding flows, whether consciously or not. Even decks that depart radically from its style often retain its underlying structure, sequencing, and narrative logic.

Using this deck allows the book to remain grounded in a symbolic language that is already widely legible, without requiring the reader to translate between multiple visual systems at once. This matters in a book concerned with structure rather than interpretation.

Fully Illustrated Minor Arcana

One of the most important reasons for using the Rider–Waite–Smith deck is its fully illustrated Minor Arcana. Earlier decks often treated the Minor Arcana as abstract arrangements of suit symbols. While historically significant, those designs offer less visual information for sustained structural study. The Rider–Waite–Smith images encode relationships, environments, motion, and constraint directly into the cards.

This allows us to study posture and stance, environment and support, tools and architecture, movement and stillness — elements that are essential for the kind of close, imagebased work this book undertakes.

Symbol Before Style

Modern decks often emphasize artistic reinterpretation, personal symbolism, or thematic cohesion. These qualities can be meaningful and powerful, but they also add layers of interpretation that can obscure underlying structure. This book works in the opposite direction.

The Rider–Waite–Smith deck was created to encode a symbolic system clearly enough that it could be taught, repeated, and transmitted. Its imagery was designed to standardize meaning rather than personalize it. This makes it especially suited to structural study — the focus remains on how symbols function, how sequences unfold, and how structure accumulates across the suits, rather than on how individual artists reinterpret those symbols. Once the system is understood, the reader is free to apply that understanding to any deck they choose.

OPENING

The Suit of Pentacles

The suit of Pentacles returns, again and again, to a single question: What can remain?

Not what can be imagined. Not what can be desired. Not what can be initiated. Pentacles attend to what can stay – what can endure within form over time, through effort, repetition, and pressure, without quietly falling apart.

This is why Pentacles are so often misunderstood. In much modern Tarot culture, they are reduced to money, work, or material success. These can certainly appear within the suit, but they are surface expressions rather than its core concern. The logic of Pentacles is older, steadier, and less interested in display.

Pentacles are oriented toward viability.

Pentacles and the Intelligence of Matter

In the Tarot, matter is not passive. It is not simply the backdrop against which life unfolds. Matter carries its own intelligence: gravity, density, resistance, limitation, and memory. Pentacles describe the moment when force meets these conditions.

Every idea, desire, or impulse eventually enters this domain if it is to last. What cannot be supported by time, energy, skill, and care does not fail morally or spiritually. It simply cannot be sustained, and so it dissolves.

Continuity Rather Than Outcome

Unlike the other suits, Pentacles are not primarily oriented toward resolution. They ask whether something can be maintained long enough to matter. Nourishment rather than inspiration. Labor rather than intention. Maintenance rather than vision. Repetition rather than breakthrough.

Pentacles care about conditions that keep life going, rather than ideas about what life could become. They ask whether a structure can continue tomorrow, and the day after that, and through the next season. In this sense, Pentacles tend toward what is practical and sustainable rather than speculative. They favor what can be carried without constant intervention. They privilege the ordinary over the exceptional.

What survives in Pentacles tends to do so quietly.

The Mythic Ground of the Suit

The symbolic roots of Pentacles lie in agrarian and household worlds: fields rather than temples, hearths rather than altars, daily provision rather than sudden revelation. This is the logic of sowing and waiting, tending rather than invoking, protecting rather than displaying.

In premodern life, survival was rarely dramatic. It was repetitive, often unglamorous, and unforgiving of excess. Pentacles preserve this memory. They hold the mythos of staying alive within limits. Pentacles value what is built up, carried forward, and maintained over time, rather than what arrives all at once through insight, inspiration, or dramatic change.

Endurance as a Form of Authority

Within Pentacles, authority does not belong to what shines brightest or moves fastest. It belongs to what lasts. This can feel unfamiliar in modern spiritual frameworks, which often associate power with visibility, expansion, or intensity. Pentacles point toward a quieter measure of value. Here, authority gathers through patience, through skill developed over time, through reliable contribution, and through the ability to sustain rather than consume. What endures does so through repetition and care.

> *Pentacles aren't interested in ambition. They're interested in sustainability.*

Agency Within the Domain of Pentacles

To recognize the Pentacles domain is not to be confined by it. People push against Pentacles all the time — by overreaching capacity, by neglecting maintenance, by choosing speed over stability, by refusing limits. Sometimes this resistance is necessary. Sometimes it carries a cost.

Pentacles don't prevent choice. They reveal the practical cost of ignoring limits. Awareness offers orientation without obligation.

How to Read the Pentacles Cards

As you move through the Pentacles cards, the questions worth holding are structural rather than personal. Is this sustainable? Is this supported? Is this effort proportional? Is this structure stable – or beginning to strain?

Some cards describe early formation. Some describe consolidation. Some describe breakdown or loss. None of them promise reward. They describe conditions.

A Final Orientation

Pentacles are not primarily occupied with meaning. They are occupied with whether meaning can be carried. This suit teaches that embodiment is not a single event, but an ongoing negotiation with time, energy, and care. To live in matter is to encounter constraint – and to discover what kind of life becomes possible within it. As you move into the individual cards, let this doctrine remain quietly in the background. You don't need to agree with it. You don't need to like it. You only need to notice when it is present.

The Pentacles will take care of the rest.

OPENING

The Cycle of Matter

Pentacles describe what happens to matter over time. The suit traces a single arc — but not in the way most modern Tarot interpretations suggest. The Ace is not a starting line. The Ten is not a finish. The numbered cards do not climb from beginning to completion in the way a story would. They turn.

What follows names that turning. Five phases describe the conditions through which any material thing must pass to endure. Each phase generates the next. The fifth produces the first. The work continues.

This is the architecture of the suit. The card chapters that follow describe individual phases of it.

Why a Cycle and Not a Sequence

Sequence implies destination. Cycle implies return. The assumption of progress — that what begins must build toward completion, and that completion is the point — is foreign to how matter actually behaves. Matter does not finish. Soil that grows a harvest must be replenished before it grows the next. A house that is built must be maintained or it falls. A skill that is learned must be practiced or it atrophies. Continuity in material form is not a state. It is a turning.

The Pentacles preserve this. What is built in the Ten does not end the suit. It becomes the conditions under which a new Ace becomes possible – not for the same person, perhaps not in the same lifetime, but within the same world, where matter continues to move whether or not anyone is watching. This is what makes the Pentacles steadier than any other suit. They do not promise resolution. They describe the turning.

The Five Phases

The phases name the conditions through which matter passes as it enters form, is held, fails, is rebuilt, and is finally inherited. Each phase covers two of the numbered cards. The two cards within a phase are not duplicates. They are different stances toward the same condition.

Arrival. Matter becomes available. A resource, a possibility, a body, a circumstance that did not exist before. Nothing is yet required of it. Nothing is yet proven. The Ace records the moment of arrival in its quietest form – matter offered without demand. The Two records arrival under load – matter that has arrived alongside what was already being carried, requiring motion to keep both upright. Arrival produces Custody: what has come must be held.

Custody. What is here must be coordinated, preserved, and protected. Stability begins to be possible. So does exclusion. Every holding draws a line, and someone falls outside the line. The Three records custody as collaboration – work coordinated within a shared structure that holds attention long enough for skill to form. The Four records custody as guard – holding tightened against loss, protection that has begun to harden into refusal. Custody produces Exposure: what is held excludes what is not.

Exposure. The holding fails for someone. Loss of access, loss of place, loss of the structure that was supposed to hold. The Five records exposure as absence – figures outside in the cold, walking past a window of warmth they cannot enter. The Six records the response to exposure – relief shaped by power, distribution measured against scales held by those who did not lose. Exposure produces Practice: what cannot be returned to must be rebuilt.

Practice. Effort becomes deliberate. The work is no longer reactive but chosen, repeated, refined. Skill begins to form, not through inspiration but through sustained contact. The Seven records practice as pause – the figure leans on his tool, looks at what has grown, and decides whether to continue. The Eight records practice as repetition – the same shape struck again and again until the worker becomes someone who can be trusted with the work. Practice produces Inheritance: what is sustained long enough begins to outlast the one who sustains it. Inheritance. What has been built begins to hold itself. It can be shared, passed forward, lived inside by others. The maker is no longer required for it to continue. The Nine records inheritance as sufficiency – a single life supported by what has been built, alone in a garden that holds. The Ten records inheritance as transmission – generations within a single frame, the house that continues after the builder is gone. Inheritance produces Arrival: what is inherited becomes the next generation's available matter.

Pairs as Stances

The pairing matters. To say that the Five and the Six are both Exposure is not to flatten them – it is to recognize that they are answering the same question from different positions. Exposure can be the experience of being outside (the Five) or the experience of receiving help on terms set by another (the Six). Both belong to the phase. Neither resolves it.

This pattern holds across the suit. The Three and the Four are both Custody, but one builds the structure and one defends it. The Seven and the Eight are both Practice, but one is the work of waiting and one is the work that builds the worker. The Nine and the Ten are both Inheritance, but one is sufficiency for a single life and one is sufficiency that has extended into a world.

> *The two cards of a phase are not duplicates. They are stances.*

Reading the suit this way changes what the cards do. A card is no longer a discrete meaning to be retrieved. It is a position within a phase, in relation to the other card that shares its position. A reader encountering the Six is encountering the Five from another angle. A reader encountering the Eight is encountering the Seven extended into time. The cards illuminate one another not because they tell a story together, but because they are different responses to the same condition.

The Courts in Relation to the Cycle

The four court cards do not occupy phases of the cycle. They sit in relation to it. They describe the persons the cycle produces.

The Page is the student of the cycle. Attention has turned toward how matter works. The Page does not yet sustain anything; the Page is at the threshold where participation becomes conscious.

The Knight is the practitioner. Continuation has become consistent enough to be relied on. The Knight is what the cycle produces when

Practice has been carried long enough to alter who the practitioner has become.

The Queen is the embodiment. Stability has matured into something that can be lived inside, cared for, extended outward. The Queen is the cycle made habitable.

The King is the governor. Stability has been organized into form that persists beyond the maker. The King is the cycle written into structures that continue without him.

These four positions are not unique to Pentacles. They name a pattern that runs through every suit and through the larger architecture of the Grist library: Becoming, Authority, Offering, Return. In the Pentacles, the pattern takes a particular form, shaped by matter and time. The Page is Pentacles in the register of Becoming – the studying, the gathering of conditions, the not-yet-required. The Knight is Pentacles in the register of Authority – sustained presence as a form of governance. The Queen is Pentacles in the register of Offering – stability extended outward as care. The King is Pentacles in the register of Return – what was carried is now organized into what can be inherited, completing the arc and producing the conditions for a new Arrival.

The courts and the cycle work together. The cycle describes what happens to matter. The courts describe what happens to the person the matter has formed.

How to Read the Suit

The chapters that follow can be read straight through, in order. They are also designed to be returned to. A reader encountering the Five may find that it sends them back to the Three, where the structure that the Five exposes was first being built. A reader sitting with the Eight may find that it sends them forward to the Knight, where the practice the Eight describes has shaped a person who can be trusted with continuation. The cards talk across the cycle, not only along it.

When a Pentacles card appears in a reading or rises into attention, the question worth holding is not only what does this card mean? but what phase is being described, and what is the other card of this phase? The phase places the card within the cycle. The other card of the phase shows what is also possible at this position — the other stance, the other response.

The cycle does not promise that any particular pass through it will succeed. Some Arrivals do not survive Custody. Some who experience Exposure do not return to Practice. Some Practices do not produce Inheritance. The cycle describes the conditions; what happens within them remains a matter of circumstance, choice, and care.

What the cycle does promise is structure. The same conditions return. The same phases recur. A reader who has learned to recognize them in one pass through the suit will recognize them again in another — and through that recognition, find that the suit's authority is not the authority of prediction. It is the authority of pattern that holds.

ARCANA LIBRARY

I

The Ace of Pentacles

FOUNDATION

The Ace of Pentacles marks a threshold: the moment when something becomes capable of existing in form. Not as an idea still moving through thought, an intention gathering shape in imagination, or an insight awaiting its context – but as something that can now be carried. This lesson is not about what should be done with that moment. It is about learning to recognize when the moment has arrived.

When Something Becomes Carryable

Before the Ace of Pentacles appears, possibilities can feel vivid, meaningful, even compelling. They may occupy thought or imagination for a long time. They may feel close, or inevitable, or long-awaited. What they are not yet is carryable. The Ace is the point where possibility acquires weight — where something now asks for time, attention, energy, and ongoing care. This doesn't mean it will succeed. It simply means it has entered a space where continuation is possible. The Tarot doesn't celebrate this transition or warn against it. It quietly names it.

A Beginning That Doesn't Rush

Unlike many beginnings, the Ace of Pentacles arrives without momentum. There is no surge forward, no urgency that demands immediate action. What has appeared will not carry itself. This can feel surprising. Beginnings are often expected to feel expansive or exciting, and the Ace of Pentacles can feel quieter than anticipated — sometimes even modest. What is present may seem ordinary, practical, or easy to overlook. It is a sign of density. The card is not withholding; it is simply showing you matter as it actually is at the moment of arrival.

> *Matter is given before it is earned.*

Availability, Not Assurance

The Ace of Pentacles is sometimes read as a guarantee — a sign that something is secure, protected, or destined to work out. The Ace does not promise security. It signals availability. Support can be built, but it is not automatic. Stability is possible, but not yet established. What has arrived can be held — or set down. The card doesn't imply danger or failure. It simply leaves the future open, which is precisely what makes the beginning real rather than predetermined.

The Reality of Cost

With the Ace of Pentacles, cost becomes part of the picture – not as a punishment or proof of misalignment, but as a natural feature of being in material form. Anything that exists materially asks for replenishment, proportionate effort, and respect for limits. Acknowledging cost doesn't diminish a beginning; it helps it remain viable. It is a description of how matter works – and an invitation to meet it honestly.

IMAGERY

The image of the Ace of Pentacles is deceptively simple. There is no figure moving forward, no gesture of action, no visible effort. Instead, the card presents a moment of suspension — something offered, not yet taken up. This stillness is not emptiness. It is the point.

I *The Ace of Pentacles*

The Offering Hand

At the center of the image, a hand emerges from a cloud, holding a single Pentacle. The hand does not grasp, push, or demand response. It offers. This gesture establishes the Ace's primary condition: matter becomes available, but not imposed. What appears can be accepted, delayed, or refused. Agency remains intact. The hand that gives does not determine what the receiver will do – it only makes the giving possible.

The Hand Without a Body

The hand that offers the Pentacle is not attached to a figure. It emerges from a cloud, and behind the cloud there is no implied person – no robe, no shoulder, no face turning toward the receiver.

This absence is the most important feature of the card. It is what distinguishes the Ace of Pentacles from every later card in the suit. From the Two onward, every figure is fully visible – engaged in juggling, building, holding, working, waiting. Material reality is mediated through human bodies. The Ace shows what comes before that mediation. Something is offered, and the source of the offering remains outside the frame.

This is not divine revelation in the dramatic sense. The hand is not glowing. There is no descending light, no choir, no lightning. The cloud is small and quiet. What the image preserves is the older mythic recognition that matter is given before it is earned – that the conditions of existence arrive without our authorship and without anyone we can thank.

The receiver, too, is not depicted. There is no figure reaching upward, no kneeling petitioner, no extended palm. The image holds the moment between giving and receiving – the offering exists, but its acceptance has not yet occurred.

The Ace records this in-between condition with deliberate exactness. The world has produced something that can be carried. No one has yet picked it up.

The Pentacle as Object

The Pentacle itself is solid, contained, and clearly defined. It is not glowing with promise or animated by force. It simply exists. This clarity distinguishes the Ace of Pentacles from other Aces. The object offered is already formed enough to carry weight. It does not represent inspiration or intention, but material presence — something that has crossed fully into form and can now be held by another hand.

The Garden and the Path

Below the offering hand lies a cultivated landscape. The garden is ordered, tended, and enclosed — not wilderness, but space shaped by prior care. The Ace does not appear in chaos. It appears where conditions already allow continuation. The flowers in the garden are specific. White lilies stand at intervals, and red poppies are scattered through the green. These are not decorative choices. The lily, in medieval iconography, is the flower of purity and beginning. The poppy is the flower of sleep, forgetting, and the dead. Their presence together names the doubled condition of any beginning — what arrives carries forgetting along with it. To enter form is also to enter the slow erosion of what came before.

Apath leads forward through the garden toward distant mountains, and its presence matters. The path suggests duration rather than destination. The Ace does not promise arrival. It indicates that movement through time is now possible, step by step, without the ground giving way.

The Archway

At the edge of the garden stands an archway, functioning as a threshold rather than a culmination. To pass through it would require movement, effort, and choice — none of which the card depicts. The Ace only shows that such a crossing can now occur without immediate collapse. This is the card's central neutrality: it does not propel. It permits.

Ground, Color, and What Is Absent

The ground in the image is stable and fertile, implying support before it has been tested. Unlike later cards in the suit, there is no strain here — only availability. This is matter before it is stressed. The palette reinforces this quality: greens dominate, suggesting life that can be sustained rather than life that is erupting. There is no urgency encoded in color or contrast. The image does not hurry. Notably, there is no human figure reaching for the Pentacle — no gesture of claiming, no sign of labor. These absences are deliberate. The Ace is not about action yet. It is about presence.

Reading the Image as Structure

Taken together, the image communicates something precise: what enters form often does so without spectacle. Support can be present before confidence arrives. Early beginnings are modest and easily overlooked. Attention and upkeep come before meaning takes shape. The image does not promise outcome. It establishes condition — and leaves everything that follows to what the receiver chooses to do with what has been placed in their hands.

TRADITION

The Ace of Pentacles carries a worldview far older than Tarot itself. It emerges from cultures where survival depended less on vision or belief and more on careful allocation — the right granting of land, tools, seed, and shelter at the right time. This card does not depict abundance. It depicts provision. What is offered is not excess but enough: enough to begin, enough to attempt continuation.

Land Granted, Not Claimed

In agrarian societies, land was rarely taken up on impulse. It was allotted — by season, by lineage, by authority, or by necessity. To receive land was not a promise of ease; it was an invitation into responsibility. What is given must be worked. What is received must be tended. What is accepted must be carried forward over time. The offering hand in the card echoes this moment of allotment precisely. The Pentacle is not seized or earned. It is placed — quietly — into the field of possibility, with everything that placement implies.

Seed Before Planting

The Ace also belongs to a moment just before action. Seed has been chosen. The ground has been prepared. The season has shifted enough to allow planting. And yet nothing has begun. This pause is not hesitation — it is attentiveness. To plant too early wastes seed. To plant too late misses the season entirely. The Ace of Pentacles occupies this narrow, careful window, when matter can enter into relationship with time without being damaged by it. The card names that window. It does not push you through it.

Household Cosmology

In subsistence households, survival depended on the careful management of stores: grain, tools, animals, fuel. Receiving supplies was rarely dramatic. It was sobering, grounding, and practical — a moment that called for accounting rather than celebration. The Ace of Pentacles carries this same tone. There is no figure of triumph here, no ceremony of arrival. The moment is quiet because the responsibility is real and familiar. This is matter that must last. And it can, if tended.

Why the Ace Is Not a Deity Card

Unlike many Tarot images, the Ace of Pentacles does not depict a named god or mythic personality. This absence is intentional. What appears here is not personal favor or divine intervention, but a structural moment — one shaped by season, land, and necessity rather than blessing alone. Matter arrives because conditions allow it, not because it has been chosen or favored. This is what gives the card its calm neutrality and its quiet weight. It simply confirms that conditions are sufficient.

> *Matter arrives because conditions allow it, not because it has been chosen or favored.*

Tradition Without Romance

Modern spiritual culture often frames beginnings as sacred, fated, or destined to succeed. The Ace of Pentacles offers a different kind of tradition — one that is not heroic, not guaranteed, and not promised to any particular outcome. Its story reflects a world where survival was uncertain, and where receiving matter meant entering obligation as much as hope. To be given something real was to be given something that would cost. That cost was not punishment. It was the shape of the gift itself. It is an honest mythology — and honesty, in a world governed by season and soil, was the only thing that kept people alive through winter.

Permission Shaped by Reality

The Ace of Pentacles is the moment when life quietly says: you may now try to remain. Nothing more. Nothing less. This is not inspiration. It is permission shaped by reality — and for something that hopes to last, that is enough.

II

The Two of Pentacles

FOUNDATION

With the Two of Pentacles, continuity becomes more complex. With the Ace, matter became available – something entered form. With the Two, that something must now be carried alongside something else. This card names the first encounter with competing demands. Not excess, not failure, not crisis. Simply the reality of managing more than one thing at a time.

From Availability to Management

The Ace of Pentacles asked a single, quiet question: Can this exist in form at all? The Two asks another: Can more than one obligation be held at the same time without something giving way? This is the first point in the Pentacles suit where balance becomes necessary — not balance as harmony or calm, but balance as active adjustment, the ongoing work of keeping multiple needs in motion. The Two of Pentacles does not describe mastery. It describes learning.

Carrying Without Consolidation

At this stage of the suit, nothing has fully settled. Resources may be present, but they are not abundant. Structures may exist, but they are not yet secure. Time is available, but already spoken for. The Two of Pentacles often appears when responsibilities overlap, when priorities shift quickly, when attention must be divided, and when trade-offs are unavoidable. This is not a sign of poor planning. It reflects the early stages of endurance.

Motion as Necessity

Unlike later Pentacles cards that emphasize steadiness, repetition, or consolidation, the Two requires movement. This movement is not ambition. It is care under constraint. What is being held cannot yet be set down. There is no stable surface available. Motion is what keeps things upright for now.

It is a phase.

> *This is balance achieved through action, not resolution.*

Strain and Choice

The Two of Pentacles introduces strain — not as punishment, but as information. Holding more than one thing at once often means energy is divided, focus must shift, rest is delayed, and mistakes become more likely. The Tarot does not judge this. It simply acknowledges it.

The Two does not ask whether this situation is ideal. It asks whether it can be sustained for the moment. And within that question, choice appears. Some things can be released. Some demands can be renegotiated. Some obligations can be postponed. The card does not instruct which choice to make. It clarifies that choice is now part of the situation. Continuing without choosing is also a choice – one that often increases strain.

The Role of the Two in the Suit

As the second card in the Pentacles sequence, the Two tests the viability the Ace made possible. Can what has begun be carried alongside what already exists? If the answer is temporarily yes, the suit continues. If the answer is no, something is released early.

It is discernment.

A Closing Orientation

The Two of Pentacles reflects a common reality: continuity is rarely simple. New things almost always arrive into lives that are already full – of responsibilities, limits, and existing commitments. The effort to keep everything moving is neither virtuous nor misguided. It is situational. This card does not promise resolution. It names the phase where adjustment is the only way forward.

IMAGERY

The image of the Two of Pentacles is among the most visibly active in the suit. Where the Ace was still, grounded, and contained, the Two is shaped by movement under pressure. Nothing in this card is at rest. Everything is in motion, and that motion is doing the work of keeping things upright. Here, preservation is not quiet. It is attentive.

II *The Two of Pentacles*

The Figure in Motion

The central figure is standing, rather than seated or supported. This detail matters. Standing requires ongoing adjustment. There is no surface to lean into, no structure to rely on. Balance must be maintained moment by moment — weight shifting, attention moving, posture continually recalibrated. This does not suggest clumsiness. It suggests effort. The Two of Pentacles does not depict incompetence. It depicts adaptation in the absence of settled structure.

The Juggled Pentacles

The two Pentacles are held in the air, connected by an infinity loop. They are not anchored to the body. They are not placed on a surface. They are not contained. This visual choice reinforces the card's central condition: nothing can yet be set down.

The infinity loop here does not signify serenity or spiritual harmony. It indicates ongoing demand. Movement must continue for balance to remain. This is balance achieved through action, not resolution.

The Absence of Grounded Support

Unlike later Pentacles cards, the ground in this image does not function as support. The figure does not root into the earth. There is no sense of solidity beneath the feet. This absence is intentional, and it distinguishes the Two from later stages in the suit, where benches, walls, tools, or stable ground begin to appear. Here, support is provisional. It exists only as long as motion is maintained.

The Sea and the Ships

In the background, ships rise and fall on uneven waves. This detail is easy to miss, but it is important. The ships are not sinking, and they are not at rest. They are navigating instability. Their presence reminds us that the figure's effort is taking place within a larger environment that is itself in motion. This is not a personal failure to balance. It is a response to shifting conditions.

The world, here, is not still.

Color and Tone

The palette of the card is lighter and more playful than many Pentacles images, which often leads to misinterpretation. The brightness does not signal ease. It reflects earlystage activity – a phase before fatigue, consequence, or consolidation has fully set in. This is what effort looks like before it has cost anything. The card carries energy because energy is required.

Clothing and Attitude

The figure's clothing is simple and practical, but not specialized. There is no armor, no apron, no tool belt. This suggests that the work being done has not yet settled into a defined role or structure. The figure is responding to circumstance rather than inhabiting a stable position. This is a temporary posture, not an identity.

What Is Absent

There is no shelter. No table. No container. No place to pause. These absences are not omissions. They communicate that this phase does not yet offer rest or consolidation. The Two of Pentacles is not a place to stay.

Reading the Image Whole

Taken together, the image conveys the same reality described in the doctrine: balance is being maintained through movement, support has not yet arrived, effort is compensating for the absence of structure, and instability is being managed, not resolved. It is holding things together long enough for something firmer to take shape.

And yet the image tells a more precise story than the word "balance" usually allows. This is balance sustained through constant attention. It can work – for a while. But it is not meant to last indefinitely. Eventually, something will need to be set down, structured, or released.

The card does not criticize the juggling. It simply shows what juggling actually asks of the one doing it.

TRADITION

The Two of Pentacles reflects a worldview shaped less by abundance than by fluctuation. Its mythic ground is not the field or the hearth, but the space between stability and loss — the place where survival depends on timing, responsiveness, and restraint rather than accumulation. This is a world where conditions change quickly, and continuity requires attention rather than certainty.

The Seafaring Cosmology

The ships in the background are not incidental. They place this card within a maritime worldview, where livelihood rose and fell with forces beyond direct human control. In such cultures, prosperity was rarely stable. Trade, weather, tides, and chance all played decisive roles in survival. The Two of Pentacles belongs to sailors, merchants, porters — those whose lives required constant adjustment rather than ownership or permanence. Here, balance is not moral or spiritual. It is practical and situational.

The Myth of the Intermediary

In many premodern societies, those who lived between worlds — land and sea, village and road, market and home — occupied an uneasy position. They were necessary. They were also exposed. The Two of Pentacles reflects this intermediary role. The figure does not belong fully to any one domain. They move between obligations, carrying resources that cannot yet be secured or settled. This is not indecision. It is liminality shaped by necessity.

Cyclical Demand Rather Than Linear Progress

The infinity loop binding the Pentacles reflects a worldview in which demands do not resolve neatly. In subsistence economies, needs rarely aligned all at once. Food, fuel, labor, and protection took turns requiring attention. What was addressed today returned tomorrow in another form. The Two of Pentacles holds this cyclical strain. There is no finish line here. Only continued adjustment until conditions shift.

Why There Is No Deity

The Two does not correspond clearly to a named god or heroic figure. This absence is worth noting. The card reflects structural reality rather than divine favor. At this stage, survival depends on attentiveness, timing, and responsiveness — not blessing. The forces shaping the situation are impersonal: weather, economy, capacity, circumstance. The Tarot does not dramatize this effort. It observes it.

The Mythic Cost of Juggling

The trickster figure appears across world mythologies — Hermes at the crossroads, Anansi weaving between powers, Coyote surviving by wit. These figures are often celebrated for their cleverness, their ability to keep many things in motion at once. The Two of Pentacles offers a quieter version of that archetype.

Here, juggling is not performance. It is what happens when resources do not yet allow rest. The myth is not about ingenuity leading to reward, but about effort required to avoid loss. This is the story of those who endure without surplus.

Transition Toward Structure

Mythically, the Two of Pentacles exists as a passage rather than a destination. It cannot be sustained indefinitely. Eventually, something must be relinquished, something must be formalized, or coordination must replace improvisation. This prepares the way for the Three of

Pentacles, where shared labor, defined roles, and stable structure begin to emerge.

> *It shows what balance looks like before anything has been built to hold it.*

Closing the Mythic Layer

The Two of Pentacles carries the memory of lives lived between tides — where survival depended on responsiveness more than security. Its myth is practical, restrained, and unsentimental.

This card does not promise balance. It shows what balance looks like before anything has been built to hold it.

ARCANA LIBRARY

III

The Three of Pentacles

FOUNDATION

In the Three of Pentacles, continuity no longer depends on constant individual effort. With the Ace, matter became available. With the Two, that matter was carried through adjustment and motion. With the Three, something new appears: structure that can be shared. This card governs the first instance in the Pentacles suit where support is no longer provisional. What was previously held through responsiveness begins to be held through form.

From Juggling to Coordination

The central shift of the Three of Pentacles is not from struggle to ease, but from improvisation to coordination. In the Two, balance was maintained through motion. In the Three, balance is maintained through relationship. Tasks are distributed. Roles begin to differentiate. Effort becomes patterned rather than reactive. This does not eliminate work. It makes work viable.

Structure as a Holding Environment

The Three of Pentacles teaches that continuity depends on environments, not just individuals. A structure is something that carries load beyond one person, remains when attention shifts elsewhere, and allows effort to be sustained without constant correction. This may take the form of shared labor, established process, or agreed-upon standards. What matters is not efficiency or harmony, but reliability.

The Three marks the first point in the suit where something can continue even if one person steps away.

Skill Within Constraint

The Three of Pentacles is often read as mastery or recognition of talent. In truth, it describes something more precise. Skill appears here not as personal excellence, but as fit — the alignment between task, capacity, and environment. Skill in Pentacles is not brilliance. It is repeatability. What works once is not yet skill. What works again and again, within limits, begins to be.

The Three acknowledges that learning occurs inside structure, not before it.

> *What works once is not yet skill. What works again and again, within limits, begins to be.*

Shared Authority

Unlike later Pentacles cards that emphasize ownership or accumulation, the Three distributes authority. No single figure in the card governs the whole. Instead, authority is relational. It emerges from coordination rather than command. This does not mean equality of power or effort. It means that continuity depends on cooperation – whether formal or informal. Authority here is functional, organized around who holds knowledge, who carries weight, and who maintains the whole.

The First Relief in the Suit

The Three of Pentacles is the first card where effort begins to ease – not because the work is lighter, but because it is better held. The body no longer needs to compensate constantly. Attention no longer needs to split endlessly. The system begins to support itself.

This relief is quiet. It is not celebration. It is the feeling of something finally having a place.

The Structural Question of the Three

The Three of Pentacles asks: Can this be carried together? Imperfectly, and with effort. But reliably enough to continue. If the answer is yes, the suit moves forward. If the answer is no, the structure must be revised or abandoned. Again, this is not moral judgment. It is structural reality.

A Closing Orientation

The Three of Pentacles does not promise success. It promises support. What has entered form can now rest, at least partially, on something other than constant personal effort. Structure has begun to hold – and with it, the suit's first quiet confirmation that what was started in the Ace may be capable of lasting.

IMAGERY

The image of the Three of Pentacles brings something entirely new to the suit. For the first time, work is taking place inside a structure. Not beside it. Not in motion between unstable conditions. But within a built environment that can hold attention, labor, and time. This shift matters.

III *The Three of Pentacles*

The Presence of Architecture

The most striking feature of the card is the architectural setting. Stone walls rise around the figures. Columns and arches frame the space. The work is not happening in open ground or shifting terrain, but inside something designed to endure.

Architecture in the Tarot does not symbolize aspiration or monumentality. It symbolizes constraint that supports. Walls limit movement, but they also bear weight. They make certain actions possible by preventing others. Here, structure does not restrict labor. It makes labor viable.

Work Within a Container

Unlike the Two of Pentacles, where nothing could be set down, the Three offers surfaces, boundaries, and defined space. Tools can be used consistently. Materials can be measured. Attention can be sustained. The environment itself participates in the work. This is the first card in the suit where effort is no longer entirely dependent on continuous adjustment. The structure absorbs some of the strain.

Multiple Figures, Distinct Roles

The Three of Pentacles is the first Pentacles card to clearly depict collaboration. The figures are not identical. They wear different clothing. They occupy different postures. Their relationship to the work is not interchangeable. This is important.

Coordination does not require sameness. It requires differentiation. Each figure contributes something specific: planning, execution, evaluation, or oversight. The image does not tell us who outranks whom. It shows that continuity depends on roles that fit together.

The Pentacles as Pattern, Not Possession

The three Pentacles are not being held, juggled, or displayed. They are embedded into the structure itself. This is a quiet but decisive shift. The Pentacles have moved from objects of attention to elements of design. They are no longer carried by individuals. They are incorporated into something larger than any one person.

Value, here, is not owned. It is integrated.

Visibility and Standards

The work in this card is visible. Plans are being consulted. Results are being assessed. Effort is occurring in shared view. Visibility brings standards. Work can now be evaluated not by personal effort alone, but by whether it fits the agreed form. Success is no longer purely subjective. It is measured against something external and shared.

The distinction matters: this is coordination, not judgment.

Grounded Support Appears

For the first time in the suit, the figures are clearly supported by ground that does not shift. They stand firmly. They do not need to compensate with constant motion. This does not mean effort disappears. It means effort can now be directed rather than dispersed. The body can settle. Attention can narrow.

What Is No Longer Needed

Notice what is absent from this image. There is no infinity loop. No waves. No sense of precarious balance. The work is still demanding, but it is no longer unstable. The Three of Pentacles marks the end of survival through motion alone.

Reading the Image Whole

Taken together, the image shows labor occurring within a holding environment, coordination replacing juggling, value embedded into form rather than carried by individuals, effort measured against shared standards, and stability sufficient for work to continue. It is foundation, not completion.

The Three of Pentacles shows the moment when something can finally be worked on rather than merely kept from falling apart. Structure has arrived — not as rigidity, but as support. What began as possibility can now be shaped.

TRADITION

The Three of Pentacles encodes a myth older than Tarot itself. It arises from worlds in which survival depended not on individual brilliance, but on craft carried forward through cooperation. In these worlds, no one person held all the knowledge required to build what endured. Structures lasted because work was distributed, learned, and upheld collectively. This card remembers that reality.

Craft as Lineage, Not Expression

In premodern societies, craft was not a personal calling. It was a lineage. Knowledge was passed hand to hand, generation to generation. Skill was not owned. It was entrusted. To work within a craft was to take up a responsibility to standards that existed before you and would continue after you. The Three of Pentacles reflects this ethic. The figures in the card are not expressing individuality. They are aligning themselves with an inherited form. The work matters not because it is new, but because it fits.

> *Skill is not owned. It is entrusted.*

Apprenticeship and Measure

The mythic foundation of the Three lies in apprenticeship. To learn a craft was to submit to constraint. One learned by repetition, correction, and observation. Progress was measured not by inspiration, but by consistency. Mistakes were expected. Deviation was corrected. Improvisation came later.

The Three of Pentacles shows work at the point where learning and execution meet. Skill is developing within form, not outside it.

Shared Authority Without Sovereignty

In many craft traditions, authority was distributed. Masters, journeymen, and apprentices each held different responsibilities, but no single figure was sovereign. Authority emerged through practice rather than decree. The Three of Pentacles encodes this relational authority. No one person controls the whole. The work itself sets the terms. Continuity depends on cooperation with both the task and one another.

Building Within Constraint

The structures associated with the Three of Pentacles were shaped by necessity, climate, and available materials. Churches, bridges, mills, workshops, and homes emerged from the intersection of what was needed and what could be sustained. Even the most elaborate ornament served function — directing water, communicating meaning, demonstrating the reliability of the guild's craft to those who would commission future work.

This is not a myth of legacy in the heroic sense. It is a myth of usefulness. What mattered was whether the structure could be relied upon by others — often people the builders would never meet.

Time as the True Collaborator

In the mythic world of the Three of Pentacles, time itself is part of the work. No structure was completed in isolation from seasons, weather, or generational labor. What endured did so because it could be maintained, repaired, and adapted by those who came later.

The Three does not promise permanence. It promises continuity through shared care.

The Cost of Cooperation

The myth of the Three is not sentimental. Shared work requires compromise. Standards limit personal preference. Individual rhythm yields to collective pace. These constraints are not punishments. They are the price of durability. The Three of Pentacles acknowledges this cost without condemning it.

Transition Toward Stability

Mythically, the Three marks the shift from survival through effort to survival through form. Something now exists that can be worked on, refined, and relied upon. The burden is no longer carried by one body alone. What follows in the suit – the question of how structure is held, defended, and eventually either preserved or released – begins here, in the quiet moment when shared craft first proves capable of lasting.

Closing the Mythic Layer

The Three of Pentacles carries the memory of hands working together under shared measure. Its myth is not about achievement. It is about fit, function, and continuation. What is being built here matters because it can be carried forward – by others, over time, within form.

ARCANA LIBRARY

IV

The Four of Pentacles

FOUNDATION

The Four of Pentacles carries a subtle but important transition in the suit. With the Three, structure became capable of holding weight. With the Four, that structure is now held onto. This card governs the moment when continuity feels secure enough to defend – but not secure enough to relax.

From Shared Support to Personal Custody

In the Three of Pentacles, stability emerged through coordination and shared standards. Responsibility was distributed. Structure belonged to the work itself. The Four changes this relationship. Here, stability becomes something that must be guarded. What was once supported collectively is now held more tightly, often by a single person or point of control. This does not mean something has gone wrong. It means the structure has become valuable enough to protect. This shift is not unique to the Four. It is what happens to any system once the cost of building it has been paid in full. Custody concentrates because the people who carried the weight of construction become the people most aware of what it took to make. The Four marks the point where that awareness turns inward. Knowing the cost of what has been built changes how it is held.

Holding as a Response to Fragility

The Four of Pentacles appears when something has been built but not yet proven durable. There is enough stability to risk loss. There is not yet enough stability to risk release. Holding arises as a rational response to this threshold. The card does not describe greed or fear by default. It describes protectiveness – the instinct to preserve what has required effort to establish.

The Shift in Effort

In earlier cards, effort was directed outward – creating, coordinating, sustaining movement. In the Four, effort turns inward. Energy is spent on maintaining boundaries, preventing loss, and limiting exposure. Movement decreases. Circulation tightens. This conserves resources – but it also reduces flexibility.

Stability Without Flow

The Four of Pentacles brings the first true stillness in the suit. But this stillness is not rest. It is containment. Resources are held rather than circulated. The structure remains intact, but growth slows. The system becomes resistant to change – not because change is impossible, but because risk feels too great.

This is stability without flow.

Capacity and Control

The Four of Pentacles is often interpreted as control. In fact, it describes something more precise: capacity under protection. The structure can now support itself, but only if conditions remain tightly managed. Control emerges not from domination, but from caution.

What looks like grasping from outside often feels like vigilance from within. The Four does not describe someone who wants more. It describes someone who has finally accumulated enough to fear what loss would cost. The earlier cards did not face this fear because they had not yet built anything that could be lost. The Four arrives precisely when something has become possible to lose for the first time. That possibility changes the body. It tightens, narrows, conserves.

The card asks: What happens if this is loosened? What might be lost? These questions are not irrational. They are transitional.

> *It describes someone who has finally accumulated enough to fear what loss would cost.*

The Structural Question of the Four

The Four of Pentacles asks: Can what has been built be protected without being constricted? At this stage, the answer is uncertain. Too much holding leads to stagnation. Too little holding risks collapse. The Four marks the tension between preservation and circulation.

A Closing Orientation

The Four of Pentacles does not condemn holding. It clarifies its cost. Protection keeps things intact – but it also limits what can enter, move, or change. This is neither right nor wrong. It is a phase in the life of structure – necessary at this point, costly if extended too long.

What follows will test whether what has been held can survive being opened, whether protection has preserved or ossified, whether the structure that was guarded is the same structure that emerges when the grip eventually loosens.

IMAGERY

The image of the Four of Pentacles is visually simple, but structurally dense. Everything in this card communicates containment. Where earlier Pentacles images showed movement, exchange, or shared structure, the Four shows stillness that has become deliberate. Nothing circulates. Nothing is offered. Nothing is set down.

IV *The Four of Pentacles*

What exists is held.

The Central Figure and Posture

The figure sits firmly, body closed around the Pentacles. Feet are planted. Arms are drawn inward. The torso leans slightly forward, enclosing what is held. This posture is not relaxed. It is bracing. The body itself has become a barrier. Stability is maintained not through environment or relationship, but through physical effort and vigilance.

This is the first card in the suit where the body is used to prevent movement rather than enable it.

Pentacles as Points of Fixation

The placement of the Pentacles is precise. One rests on the head. One is held tightly against the chest. Two are secured beneath the feet. Each placement corresponds to a form of holding: thought constrained, feeling guarded, movement restricted. The Pentacles are no longer integrated into structure, as they were in the Three. They are no longer in motion, as in the Two. They are isolated and defended.

Value is no longer embedded. It is possessed.

The Absence of Exchange

There are no other figures present. No collaborators. No witnesses. No recipients. The figure is alone with what is being protected. This isolation is important. The Four of Pentacles marks the point where stability feels personal rather than shared. Protection has narrowed from coordination to custody. Continuity now depends on exclusion.

Ground and Seat as False Rest

The figure appears seated, suggesting rest – but the image contradicts this impression. The seat is rigid. The posture is tense. The hands grip rather than rest. This is not repose. It is holding still. The body cannot relax because release feels risky. Stillness here is maintained through effort, not ease.

The City in the Distance

Behind the figure, a city stands. This detail is often overlooked. The city represents systems of circulation — trade, exchange, relationship, shared life. It is visible, but distant. The figure is positioned outside it, turned away from participation. The structure exists. The figure has withdrawn from it.

This reinforces the card's theme: stability preserved by separation rather than engagement.

Color and Compression

The palette is muted and heavy. There is little air in the image. Little openness. The colors compress the space, reinforcing the sense that everything is drawn inward and downward. The image feels contained because it is.

What Is Absent

There is no movement. No exchange. No visible pathway forward. Unlike earlier Pentacles cards, there is no suggestion of progression or development. The structure is intact — but static.

Reading the Image Whole

Taken together, the image shows value held rather than circulated, stability maintained through vigilance, protection replacing coordination, stillness that requires effort, and separation from shared systems. It is contraction.

The Four of Pentacles is often read as greed or fear. The image tells a more careful story. This is what holding looks like when something has become too valuable to risk — and not yet stable enough to release. Nothing is wrong here. But nothing is moving.

TRADITION

The Four of Pentacles carries a myth shaped by scarcity remembered, not scarcity imagined. It arises from cultures where loss was not theoretical and security, once gained, could disappear quickly. In such worlds, holding was not a flaw of character. It was a survival strategy learned through experience. This card remembers that logic.

Wealth as Vulnerability

In premodern societies, possession increased exposure. To have grain, land, tools, or coin was to become visible — to neighbors, to authorities, to thieves, to obligation. Wealth did not guarantee safety. It often increased risk.

The Four of Pentacles reflects this tension. What has been accumulated now requires protection. Value attracts attention. Security creates something that can be taken. Holding emerges not from excess, but from awareness of loss.

The Myth of the Watcher

Across myth and folklore, there are figures who guard rather than build: keepers of gates, treasurers, wardens, household heads. These figures are rarely celebrated. They are necessary, cautious, and often solitary. Their role is not expansion, but preservation. The Four of Pentacles belongs to this lineage. The figure does not create new wealth. They ensure what exists does not disappear. Their vigilance maintains continuity — but at the cost of isolation.

Hoarding Before Hoarding Was a Sin

In modern culture, hoarding is moralized. Historically, it was contextual. To store grain before winter, to keep tools close, to limit sharing when survival was uncertain – these were not acts of greed. They were acts of calculation shaped by lived experience.

The Four of Pentacles encodes this older ethic. The question was not should one hold, but how long can one afford to release?

Boundary as Protection

Mythically, the Four represents the moment when boundary becomes central. Walls, locks, chests, guarded rooms – all appear in folklore at points where something valuable must be preserved against threat. These boundaries protect life, lineage, and continuity. But they also restrict flow.

The Four of Pentacles remembers both sides of boundary-making: safety gained, movement lost.

Fear Is Not the Whole Story

Although fear may be present in this card, it is not its sole driver. More often, the Four of Pentacles reflects memory – of instability, of loss narrowly avoided, of effort required to build what now exists. Holding is informed by history. The card does not ask whether fear is justified. It shows how protection becomes habitual.

The Cost of Guarded Continuity

In myth, guardians often become fixed in place. Their watch preserves what matters, but it also prevents change. Over time, protection hardens into refusal. The gatekeeper forgets why the gate exists. The Four of Pentacles sits at this threshold. Holding is still functional – but it is beginning to limit what can enter, circulate, or grow.

Preparing the Way for Loss

Mythically, the Four does not last. What is held too tightly eventually encounters pressure it cannot withstand — economic, environmental, or relational. The guarded structure becomes brittle. This is the pattern that recurs across cultures: the fortress that cannot bend, the treasury that cannot circulate, the boundary that becomes a cage.

The Four is not the fall. It is the moment before it.

> *It asks when holding begins to replace living.*

Closing the Mythic Layer

The Four of Pentacles carries the myth of those who survived by guarding what they had. Its story is not one of vice. It is one of caution shaped by experience.

This card does not condemn holding. It asks when holding begins to replace living.

V

The Five of Pentacles

FOUNDATION

With the Five of Pentacles, continuity ruptures. With the Four, stability was held tightly, protected through vigilance and boundary. With the Five, that protection fails — or is no longer sufficient. This card governs moments when support is absent, not because effort was lacking, but because conditions have changed beyond what holding can manage.

From Holding to Exposure

The central shift of the Five of Pentacles is not loss of value, but loss of access. What mattered still matters. What was needed is still needed. What is gone is support.

The Five does not indicate moral failure, poor planning, or lack of worth. It names the experience of exposure — being without shelter, without resource, without inclusion in systems that once sustained life.

> *What mattered still matters. What was needed is still needed. What is gone is support.*

Scarcity as Structural Condition

In the Pentacles suit, scarcity is not psychological. It is environmental. The Five describes conditions in which resources are insufficient, access is blocked, systems exclude rather than support, and effort no longer yields stability. This is not a temporary juggling problem like the Two. It is not cautious holding like the Four.

Something essential is missing.

The Experience of Being Outside

The imagery of the Five places figures outside — in cold, darkness, or movement through inhospitable space. But this matters more than the emotional tone. The Five governs situations where continuity exists elsewhere but is not available to you. Shelter, warmth, or stability may exist nearby, but not within reach.

This is the pain of exclusion rather than annihilation.

Loss Without Resolution

The Five of Pentacles does not promise recovery. It does not offer reassurance that things will improve quickly. Its role in the suit is diagnostic, not redemptive. This is the card that names what happens when systems fail to carry everyone. Endurance here is not productive. Effort does not resolve the condition. This distinguishes the Five from earlier Pentacles cards, where effort could still preserve continuity.

The Limits of Self-Sufficiency

The Five of Pentacles exposes a structural truth: no one survives alone indefinitely. Where earlier cards dealt with individual capacity – holding, juggling, guarding – the Five reveals the limits of those strategies. When environment withdraws support, personal effort cannot compensate. This is not weakness. It is reality.

What the Five Asks

The Five of Pentacles asks no questions about attitude, belief, or resilience. It asks one thing: What happens when continuity is no longer accessible through existing structures?

The answer is not contained in the Five itself. This card does not solve the condition it names. What follows in the suit – the question of redistribution, assistance, and unequal power – begins here, in the recognition that self-sufficiency has reached its limit.

A Closing Orientation

The Five of Pentacles is not a card of punishment. It is a card of absence. Absence of shelter. Absence of resource. Absence of access. The suit does not turn away from this reality. It records it plainly – and in doing so, it honors the experience of those who find themselves outside without pretending that naming the condition is the same as resolving it.

IMAGERY

The image of the Five of Pentacles is stark, but it is not chaotic. Everything in this card is arranged to show absence in relation to presence – what exists nearby but is not accessible.

V *The Five of Pentacles*

Figures in Motion, Not at Rest

The figures in the Five of Pentacles are moving. They are not seated. They are not working. They are not sheltered. Movement here does not indicate progress. It indicates necessity. They walk because stopping offers no support. There is nowhere to rest.

This distinguishes the Five from earlier Pentacles cards. The Two moved to maintain balance. The Three worked within structure. The Four held still to protect. The Five moves because stillness would worsen exposure.

The Lack of Grounded Support

Unlike earlier Pentacles images, the ground here does not offer stability. Snow covers the surface. Footing is cold and unreliable. The ground does not hold; it drains energy. Each step costs more than it gives. This is a visual language of environmental hostility — not emotional despair. The problem is not internal. It is structural.

The Window as Structural Contrast

The stained-glass window dominates the background. It is the card's central contrast. Inside the window: light, order, warmth, and symbolic wealth. Outside the window: cold, darkness, movement without shelter. What matters is proximity. Support exists. Structure exists. Continuity exists. But it is not available to those in the foreground.

The Five of Pentacles is not about total absence — it is about exclusion.

Pentacles as Distant Symbol

The Pentacles appear in the window, not with the figures. They are present as symbols of value and structure, but removed from lived access. This reinforces the card's core condition: what sustains life exists, but cannot be reached or received. Value has become abstract. It no longer circulates.

Bodies Under Strain

The figures' bodies show damage and fatigue. One is injured. Both are poorly clothed. Movement is uneven. It is consequence. Exposure leaves marks. Lack accumulates in the body over time. The image records this plainly without embellishment.

Absence of Interaction

The figures do not look toward the window. They do not knock. They do not appeal. They do not turn inward toward each other dramatically. This detail matters. The image does not depict rescue or refusal. It shows people moving within conditions where access is not assumed and appeal may not be possible.

Color and Compression

The palette is muted and cold. Blues, greys, and whites dominate. There is little warmth in the figures themselves. Light exists only behind glass. The visual effect reinforces separation: warmth is contained elsewhere.

What Is Absent

There is no doorway. No hand extended. No visible exchange. The image offers no immediate solution. This is not because help is impossible, but because this card is not the place where help arrives.

Reading the Image Whole

Taken together, the image shows movement driven by lack rather than choice, environmental conditions that drain rather than support, proximity to structure without access, value visible but unavailable, and bodies bearing the cost of exclusion. It is deprivation.

The Five of Pentacles does not sentimentalize suffering. It shows what scarcity looks like when systems fail to include everyone. The light remains inside. The Pentacles remain intact. What is missing is access.

TRADITION

The Five of Pentacles carries a myth shaped not by failure, but by exclusion. It belongs to worlds where survival depended on access to shared structures – guilds, churches, households, kinship networks, stores of food and fuel. To fall outside these systems was not a private misfortune. It was a material condition with immediate consequences.

This card remembers what happens when continuity exists, but not for everyone.

Poverty as Disconnection, Not Defect

In premodern societies, poverty was rarely understood as a personal flaw. More often, it arose from rupture – loss of land or trade, injury or illness, widowhood or exile, debt, displacement, or failed harvest.

The Five of Pentacles reflects this reality. The figures are not empty-handed because they are unworthy. They are outside because connection has been broken. The myth here is not one of moral failure, but of severed support.

The Threshold That Does Not Open

Across folklore and religious myth, there are moments when doors remain closed. Temples, monasteries, guild halls, and houses all functioned as centers of protection – but only for those who belonged. The poor, the sick, the foreign, and the indebted often stood at the edge of these spaces.

The Five of Pentacles encodes this threshold. Light and order exist behind glass. The system is intact. But entry is not automatic. Belonging determines who is sheltered and who is exposed.

Charity Without Assurance

Historically, aid was uneven and conditional. Religious institutions offered alms — but often selectively. Guilds supported members, not strangers. Households fed their own first. Survival depended on proximity, reputation, and timing. The Five of Pentacles does not depict generosity or refusal. It depicts uncertainty — when help might exist, but cannot be assumed.

This is the myth of waiting in the cold without guarantee.

Suffering Without Meaning

Unlike many spiritual narratives, the Five of Pentacles does not frame suffering as instructive, redemptive, or transformative. There is no lesson promised here. No purification. No moral arc. The myth simply records that deprivation hurts — and that endurance alone does not restore what has been lost. This refusal to spiritualize suffering is part of the card's honesty.

The Social Cost of Exclusion

In mythic terms, the Five represents what happens when structures protect themselves at the expense of those who fall outside them. Walls preserve what is inside. They also create an outside. The Five of Pentacles stands in that outside space, holding the knowledge that survival is not distributed evenly — even in worlds that claim order, faith, or justice.

What the Five Exposes

Mythically, the Five does not resolve its own condition. It exposes it. By naming absence and exclusion, the card raises the questions that the rest of the suit must now contend with: Who has access? Who decides? On what terms? These are not rhetorical questions. They are the ground on which everything that follows in the suit is built.

> *This card does not explain suffering. It names the structures that allow it.*

Closing the Mythic Layer

The Five of Pentacles carries the memory of standing near warmth without being able to enter. Its myth is not tragic. It is exact.

This card does not explain suffering. It names the structures that allow it.

ARCANA LIBRARY

VI

The Six of Pentacles

FOUNDATION

The Six of Pentacles brings a return of resources – but not a return to equality. With the Five, support was absent or inaccessible. With the Six, support exists again. What has changed is not scarcity itself, but distribution. This card governs moments when continuity is restored through asymmetrical exchange: some have, some lack, and support moves across that divide.

From Absence to Allocation

The central shift of the Six of Pentacles is the reappearance of circulation. Resources are no longer entirely withheld. Something is being given, received, or redistributed. But this circulation does not occur evenly or reciprocally. One party controls access. Another depends on it.

This is not yet balance. It is relief shaped by hierarchy.

Support With Conditions

The Six of Pentacles introduces a structural truth: help is rarely neutral. Aid is shaped by power, timing, discretion, and judgment. Whether intentional or not, the one who gives determines when support is offered, how much is given, under what terms, and whether it can be withdrawn. The Tarot does not frame this as cruelty or kindness. It names it as structure.

> *Help is rarely neutral.*

The Source of the Asymmetry

The asymmetry in the Six is not accidental. It is the consequence of what happened in the cards before it. The Four held resources tightly enough to preserve them. The Five exposed who fell outside that holding. By the Six, the structure that was guarded in the Four has begun to release small portions of what it kept – but it releases them according to its own logic, on its own terms.

This is why the Six cannot be read as simple generosity. The conditions that made giving necessary were created by the conditions that made giving rare. The same accumulation that enabled the Four's protection produced the Five's exclusion and now produces the Six's selective relief. The exchange feels uneven because the situation that requires the exchange is itself uneven.

The Six does not invent the imbalance. It distributes it.

Dependency Without Collapse

Unlike the Five, where lack is absolute, the Six allows continuity to resume. Needs are met enough to survive. The system does not collapse. But dependency arrives. Receiving support means living inside another's capacity or willingness. Stability here is real — but provisional.

The Scale as Measure, Not Justice

The scales often depicted in the Six do not promise fairness in a moral sense. They measure proportion. The Six asks: How much is given? To whom? By whom? The scales measure proportion, not the justice of equality. They name the logic of managed imbalance.

Giving and Receiving as Roles

In the Six of Pentacles, giving and receiving are roles — not identities, but positions within a moment. One may give in one context and receive in another. What matters is not character, but placement within the structure of exchange. The card does not guarantee dignity. It does not guarantee exploitation. It simply names that continuity is now mediated by unequal access.

The Structural Question of the Six

The Six of Pentacles asks: What happens when survival depends on another's discretion? This question applies to both sides of the exchange. For the receiver, it asks what is required to accept support. For the giver, it asks what responsibility accompanies control. The Six does not answer these questions. It exposes them.

A Closing Orientation

The Six of Pentacles is not a card of generosity. It is a card of relief shaped by power. Support has returned, but not without structure. Continuity is possible again — but only through managed exchange.

The imbalance named here is not resolved by the Six itself. That work – the slow movement toward self-reliance, disciplined effort, and earned stability – belongs to what follows.

It is the beginning of negotiation.

IMAGERY

The image of the Six of Pentacles is one of the clearest depictions of hierarchy in the suit. Everything in this card is arranged vertically: standing and kneeling, holding and receiving, measuring and waiting. The structure of the exchange is visible at a glance.

VI *The Six of Pentacles*

The asymmetry is the subject.

The Central Figure: Standing Authority

The standing figure occupies the highest position in the image. They are upright, clothed, and stable. Their posture is relaxed. They are not braced or strained. Their feet are firmly planted, and their body is not engaged in effort. This figure does not need to move to maintain stability.

Support, here, belongs to position.

The Scale: Measure, Not Equality

The scale held by the standing figure is often interpreted as justice or fairness. In fact, it represents control of measure. The scale does not ensure balance between people. It determines how much is given, when, and to whom. The one who holds the scale controls proportion. This is not a moral claim. It is a structural fact.

The Act of Giving

Coins are extended downward from the standing figure's hand. This direction matters. Giving flows from above to below. The transaction is one-directional. The giver does not receive anything in return within the image. This reinforces the asymmetry of the relationship. Circulation has resumed — but it is not reciprocal.

The Kneeling Figures

The two receiving figures are positioned lower in the image. They kneel rather than stand. Their posture suggests dependency — not submission as character, but submission as circumstance. Their bodies are engaged in reaching rather than holding. They do not control the exchange. They await it.

Importantly, the two figures are not identical. This suggests that receiving itself is not uniform. Even among those who lack, access may differ.

Ground and Stability

The ground beneath the standing figure appears stable. The ground beneath the kneeling figures is less defined. This contrast reinforces the card's core condition: some stand on secure footing, others rely on assistance to remain upright at all. Stability is not evenly distributed.

Clothing and Resource

The standing figure's clothing is intact and complete. The receiving figures are more simply dressed, possibly worn. This visual difference is not aesthetic. It indicates unequal access to resources over time. One figure has surplus; others do not. The image does not explain why. It simply shows the result.

Absence of Mutual Gaze

There is little eye contact between figures. This is important. The exchange is functional, not relational. There is no visible negotiation, gratitude, or acknowledgment. The interaction is mediated by role rather than relationship. This reinforces the card's logic.

What Is Absent

There is no table. No shared surface. No mutual exchange. It is allocation, not collaboration.

Reading the Image Whole

Taken together, the image shows vertical hierarchy rather than horizontal exchange, control of measure residing with the giver, dependency without collapse, relief without equality, and stability mediated by discretion. It is managed imbalance, not cruelty.

The Six of Pentacles is often read as generosity. The image tells a more exact story. Support has returned – but it is controlled. Relief exists – but it is conditional. Circulation resumes – but on unequal ground. This card does not ask whether this is fair. It shows how support moves when power is uneven.

TRADITION

The Six of Pentacles carries a myth shaped by worlds in which survival depended not only on work, but on access to those who controlled surplus. It arises from social orders where resources accumulated unevenly, and where continuity for many required the intervention of a few. In such worlds, generosity was never abstract. It was personal, visible, and conditional.

This card remembers that reality.

Charity as Structure, Not Sentiment

In premodern societies, charity was not primarily an expression of compassion. It was an institution. Religious almsgiving, noble patronage, guild assistance, and household provision all functioned as structured systems that redistributed resources downward while preserving hierarchy. Aid relieved suffering – but it also reinforced existing power arrangements. The Six of Pentacles reflects this dual function. Support restores continuity. It does not erase inequality.

The Patron and the Dependent

The mythic figures behind the Six are patrons and dependents. The patron controlled land, coin, food, or protection. The dependent relied on this control to survive. Gratitude was expected. Loyalty was often implied. Independence was limited by access. This relationship was not always cruel. It was often necessary. But it was never neutral.

The Six of Pentacles encodes this tension without resolving it.

Mercy With Measure

In myth and history, mercy was rarely boundless. Alms were weighed. Recipients were assessed. Limits were imposed. The scale in the Six reflects this logic: generosity measured, not overflowing. Enough is given to sustain life, not enough to overturn the system that requires giving in the first place.

This is mercy shaped by preservation of order.

Obligation Flows Both Ways

The Six of Pentacles myth does not belong only to the receiver. The giver, too, is bound. Those who controlled surplus were expected to give – or risk unrest, moral condemnation, or divine judgment. Charity functioned as social glue. Withholding entirely threatened the stability of the whole. Thus, the giver's position carries responsibility as well as power. The card holds both sides of this obligation.

The Visibility of Giving

Charity in older cultures was often public. Coins were distributed openly. Recipients were seen. Hierarchies were reinforced through display. The Six of Pentacles reflects this visibility. The act of giving is not private. It is witnessed and structured. This reinforces roles and clarifies position. Support is not anonymous. It is situational.

Relief Without Liberation

Mythically, the Six of Pentacles does not promise escape. It offers reprieve. Life continues. Hunger is eased. Shelter may be regained. But the conditions that produced scarcity remain intact. It is the limit of what generosity alone can do.

> *The Six does not invent the imbalance. It distributes it.*

Closing the Mythic Layer

The Six of Pentacles carries the memory of mercy offered from above. Its myth is neither benevolent nor cruel. It is exact. The Six provides time – not resolution. What follows in the suit must be built from something other than the giver's discretion.

This card asks not whether giving is good, but how survival is shaped when access is unequal.

ARCANA LIBRARY

VII

The Seven of Pentacles

FOUNDATION

The Work of Waiting

The Seven of Pentacles is the first pause in the suit. After the circulation of the Six — where resources moved unevenly but urgently — the Seven introduces stillness. Not rest, but evaluation. Something has been invested, effort has been applied, and now the question becomes whether continuation is justified. This card governs moments when action gives way to appraisal.

From Circulation to Assessment

With the Six, resources moved in response to need and imbalance. With the Seven, movement slows. The work has been done – at least enough to produce visible result. What remains is to decide whether what has been started is worth sustaining. It is discernment, not doubt.

Labor Without Immediate Return

The Seven of Pentacles belongs to phases where effort has been expended, but reward has not yet materialized in full. Growth exists, but it is incomplete. Return is possible, but delayed. The card does not promise success and does not signal failure. It records a moment where continuation requires choice rather than momentum.

Patience as Structural Necessity

Patience in the Seven of Pentacles is not a virtue to cultivate. It is a condition imposed by time. Certain processes cannot be hurried without damage, and assessment must occur before further investment. This is not resignation – it is care for what already exists. The Tarot does not reward waiting here. It acknowledges it.

Evaluation Without Rejection

The Seven permits evaluation without requiring abandonment. Something may be continued, adjusted, or eventually released – but none of that happens yet. The card holds the moment of looking clearly before deciding. This is not the anxiety of indecision. It is the seriousness of stewardship.

Energy and Return

At this stage of the suit, energy becomes precious. Effort is no longer free-flowing, and every additional act carries cost. The Seven asks whether further labor will strengthen what has begun — or exhaust it. It is a question of proportionality.

The Structural Question of the Seven

The Seven of Pentacles asks: is what I am tending capable of becoming worth the effort required to maintain it? Not immediately. Not eventually. But structurally. This question is neither optimistic nor pessimistic. It is responsible.

> *Knowing when to withdraw is as important as knowing when to persist.*

A Closing Orientation

The Seven of Pentacles is not about waiting for reward. It is about deciding whether waiting makes sense. This card honors the intelligence of pause — the moment when effort is temporarily withheld so that judgment can form. As the midpoint of the suit, it serves as a hinge: everything that follows depends on what is decided here.

IMAGERY

The image of the Seven of Pentacles is one of the quietest in the suit. After the motion of the Two, the exchange of the Six, and the strain of uneven support, the figure in the Seven stops moving. Tools are set aside. The body leans. Attention turns toward what has grown.

VII *The Seven of Pentacles*

Nothing is being done. Something is being weighed.

The Figure at Rest

The figure stands still, supported by their tool. The body is upright but not active. There is no strain, no urgency. Weight is distributed evenly, suggesting a pause that is intentional rather than forced.

This posture is unique in the suit. Every previous figure has been engaged — juggling, building, guarding, walking, giving, or receiving. The Seven is the first card where the body is permitted to stop without that stopping being a crisis. It is assessment, not exhaustion.

The Tool as Anchor

The staff or tool held by the figure functions as support rather than instrument. It is no longer being used to work the field. Instead, it anchors the body while attention shifts away from labor and toward evaluation.

The figure has not abandoned the tool or set it down entirely — they are leaning into it. The body's weight rests on support rather than driving action.

Work has been done. Work is not currently happening.

The Pentacles on the Vine

The Pentacles appear arranged on a growing plant. They are not scattered across a surface or held by a figure. They are embedded in a living process — attached to something that is still developing.

The crop cannot yet be harvested. The vine still requires time. Unlike the Three, where Pentacles were integrated into architectural structure, or the Four, where they were clutched against the body, here they belong to something organic and incomplete. Value is present but not yet realized.

Distance and Perspective

The figure stands apart from the plant. The person is not immersed in the growth. They are observing it from a position that allows the whole to be seen.

In earlier cards, figures were embedded in their situations — inside architecture, surrounded by snow, positioned within exchange. The Seven creates separation between the person and the condition.

Perspective has replaced action.

Ground and Stability

The ground beneath the figure is solid and even. The figure is not struggling to remain upright. The earth supports standing and standing supports looking. In the Two, the ground offered nothing — motion was the only option. In the Five, the ground drained rather than supported. Here, the ground holds. But what grows from it remains uncertain.

Color and Tone

The palette of the Seven is muted and earthy — greens, browns, and subdued golds. There is no urgency conveyed through color. No warmth suggesting comfort. No cold suggesting deprivation. The image feels suspended between effort and outcome, occupying a visual register that refuses to signal either hope or discouragement.

The colors do not tell the viewer how to feel about what they are seeing. They present conditions and wait.

What Is Absent

There is no harvest basket. No gesture of celebration. No sign of abundance or loss. No other figures. No exchange. No motion.

The image resists conclusion. The Seven does not show what comes next. It shows the moment before that decision is made.

Reading the Image Whole

Taken together, the image shows effort temporarily withheld, growth present but incomplete, distance enabling evaluation, stability without guarantee, and patience imposed by process rather than chosen as virtue. The figure is not waiting with faith. They are looking with care. And what they decide here will determine whether labor resumes or something is quietly released.

TRADITION

The Seven of Pentacles arises from a mythic worldview shaped by the rhythms of cultivation – planting, tending, waiting, assessing. These rhythms coexisted alongside conquest and conflict, but they operated by a different logic. Where battle rewarded decisive action, agriculture rewarded patience and discernment. The Seven belongs to this second logic. Its truth predates modern productivity: not all effort should be continued simply because it has begun.

The Farmer's Pause

In agrarian life, there were moments when labor ceased – not because the work was finished, but because intervention would do more harm than good. Fields were planted. Vines were trained. Seed had taken root. At this stage, further disturbance could damage growth rather than accelerate it. The wise farmer learned to pause, observe, and decide whether the crop was worth continued investment. The Seven of Pentacles encodes this pause.

Time as an Active Force

In mythic and premodern cosmologies, time was not neutral. It acted. Growth depended on seasons, weather, soil, and unseen processes beneath the surface. Human effort could not override these forces. It could only cooperate – or exhaust itself fighting them. The Seven of Pentacles reflects respect for this reality. Waiting here is not submission. It is alignment with processes that cannot be rushed.

Stewardship Rather Than Hope

The myth behind the Seven is not one of optimism. It is one of responsibility. Stewardship meant evaluating whether land, animals, or crops could justify further labor. Resources were finite, and energy spent in one place could not be spent elsewhere. Continuing blindly was dangerous. Abandoning too quickly was wasteful. The Seven holds the tension between these risks.

> *Stewardship rather than hope.*

Delayed Return Without Guarantee

Harvest was never assured. Drought, blight, pests, or conflict could undo months of labor. The Seven of Pentacles reflects this uncertainty — growth visible today did not guarantee yield tomorrow. This is why the figure in the card does not celebrate. They assess.

The Ethics of Withdrawal

Mythically, the Seven also carries the permission to stop. Fields could be left fallow. Projects could be abandoned. Effort could be redirected. This was not failure. It was survival. The Seven of Pentacles preserves this ethic: knowing when to withdraw is as important as knowing when to persist.

A Card Without Deity

Like much of the Pentacles suit, the Seven does not belong to a god of harvest or fertility. This absence matters. The card reflects a worldview in which continuation depended less on blessing than on discernment. The forces at play were seasonal and material, not personal or divine. The Tarot does not mythologize success here. It mythologizes judgment.

Closing the Mythic Layer

The Seven of Pentacles carries the memory of those who learned to pause without despair. Its myth is quiet, unsentimental, and deeply practical. This card does not promise reward. It offers clarity about whether reward is still worth pursuing – and in that clarity, the entire direction of the suit is decided.

VIII

The Eight of Pentacles

FOUNDATION

The Eight of Pentacles brings a decisive shift to the suit. Up to this point, the cards have been concerned with conditions: the arrival of something into form, the effort required to carry it, the ways it must be balanced, protected, supported, and endured. Each stage has asked whether continuation is possible under a given set of circumstances. With the Eight, that question changes. Continuation is no longer uncertain. It has become deliberate.

From Endurance to Practice

In earlier stages of the Pentacles sequence, effort is situational – arising in response to pressure, necessity, or opportunity. Attention may be divided. Results may be inconsistent. Even in the Seven, where patience becomes central, the emphasis remains on waiting.

The Eight moves beyond this. Something is no longer simply present. It is being practiced. This distinction is fundamental. Practice implies repetition that is chosen and sustained — not reactive, not occasional, and not dependent on changing conditions. The figure in the card is not testing the work or considering it. They are doing it again, and then again, and then again. This repetition is not stagnation. It is the mechanism through which form becomes reliable.

A Different Relationship to Time

Practice creates a different relationship to time. Earlier in the suit, time functioned as a condition to be endured or waited through. Here, time becomes the medium through which change is produced. Each return to the same action refines perception, reduces hesitation, and increases coordination. The person engaged in the work does not remain unchanged — not through insight or sudden understanding, but through sustained contact with the task itself.

Skill as Product, Not Precondition

The Eight of Pentacles is often read as a card of talent or mastery. In truth, it describes something more precise. Skill here is not inherent. It is built. It emerges from repetition carried long enough that body, mind, and material begin to align. What once required conscious effort becomes more familiar. Not effortless, but workable.

This is why the Eight carries so little sense of spectacle. There is no visible milestone, no clear marker of achievement. The work may feel repetitive, even tedious. It may lack external validation. And yet it is precisely this kind of effort that produces the most stable forms of change.

> *Skill, here, is not inherent. It is built.*

Commitment Without Compulsion

The Eight does not remove choice. Nothing forces continuation. The work could be abandoned. Attention could be withdrawn. This is what makes the stage meaningful — skill develops only where participation is allowed to persist. The card does not assume permanence. It observes commitment in motion.

The Structural Question of the Eight

The Eight of Pentacles asks: will sustained contact with this work be allowed to continue long enough for ability to form?

The earlier cards ask whether something can exist, be carried, be supported, and endured. The Eight asks whether endurance will now become transformation — not symbolic transformation, but functional. The kind that alters what can be reliably done, and therefore what can be sustained.

A Closing Orientation

The Eight of Pentacles does not measure progress. It recognizes where repetition is already at work — in routines, in practices returned to, in efforts that feel ordinary but continue anyway. Repetition alters capacity. It changes what can be done without strain, what can be sustained over time, and what can be relied upon.

What matters here is not speed, and not visible improvement. What matters is that contact has been maintained. And in that maintenance, something has begun to change.

IMAGERY

The Tree, the Workbench, and the Path Back to the World

The Eight of Pentacles depicts a craftsperson seated outdoors, engraving a pentacle with careful attention. Nothing about the scene is rushed. The figure leans forward, fully engaged in the precise work of forming the symbol. Above and beside them, completed pentacles are mounted vertically on a thick wooden beam.

VIII *The Eight of Pentacles*

This is the first card in the suit where effort is neither reactive nor evaluative. It is simply ongoing.

The Tree Trunk

At first glance, the beam holding the completed pentacles appears to be a simple post. Closer inspection reveals something more specific. This is not milled lumber. It is a tree trunk — its rings visible, its form intact, not fully separated from its origin. The pentacles are not hung on an artificial structure. They are mounted directly onto what was once living growth. This detail matters. The symbols of human skill are fastened to the record of natural time. Both are forms of accumulation — one biological, one deliberate. The tree grew by adding layers, each ring marking a completed cycle. The pentacles reflect the same logic. Each one represents a single act of repetition successfully completed. Together, they show skill not as a singular achievement, but as something layered. Built cycle by cycle.

The Bench and the Tree Share the Same Origin

The craftsperson sits on a bench made from the same wood as the display beam. One portion supports the body. Another displays the results of skill. This suggests a continuity between support and achievement — the work does not emerge from nowhere. It emerges from what has already existed long enough to be shaped. The figure is literally supported by the same material that now holds their completed work.

This reinforces one of the Eight's central themes: skill develops through continuity, not isolation. The past becomes the structure that allows present capability.

The Town and the Path

In the distance, behind the craftsperson, a town is visible. A clear path leads toward it. This is not an incidental background detail. The craftsperson has stepped outside the town — they are not currently participating in its life. But the path remains open.

This suggests that skill is developed in separation but exists for reintegration. The town represents the social world where skill becomes meaningful, where it is exchanged, where it sustains life. The path confirms that this stage is temporary. Apprenticeship happens outside. Application happens within.

The Position of the Body

The craftsperson's posture reinforces this transitional state. They are seated, stable, and grounded. One pentacle rests in their hands. Another lies near their feet. Several more are completed and mounted. The arrangement shows progression – work underway, work completed, work yet to be formed. This places the figure inside an ongoing process rather than at its beginning or end.

The Absence of Audience

No one watches. No one supervises. No one evaluates. This absence is deliberate. Skill develops through attention, not recognition. The card does not show success. It shows formation. This distinguishes the Eight from later Pentacles cards, where skill has already shaped independence and stability. Here, the focus remains on the act itself.

Reading the Image Whole

Every element of the card reinforces the same truth: skill grows through continuity. The tree trunk shows natural accumulation. The mounted pentacles show human accumulation. The bench shows support drawn from the same source. The distant town shows the future context where skill will matter. The path shows that this work leads somewhere real.

The Eight of Pentacles shows the stage where repetition begins to leave permanent marks. The figure is no longer beginning and no longer evaluating. They are building capability through sustained contact with the work. Like the tree rings beside them, their skill is becoming part of their structure.

TRADITION

Skill, Apprenticeship, and the Myth of Becoming Capable

The Eight of Pentacles belongs to a world where survival depended on learned skill. Not instinct. Not inspiration. Practice. This card encodes a reality older than Tarot itself: the understanding that capability is built slowly, through repetition, under conditions that cannot be rushed. It reflects a time when knowing how to make something was the difference between continuity and collapse.

The Apprenticeship Worldview

In premodern societies, skill was not assumed. It was transmitted. A person became capable through apprenticeship – years spent repeating the same actions under careful attention. This repetition was not considered limitation. It was considered initiation. The apprentice did not begin as a master and gradually reveal their nature. They began as unskilled and were slowly reshaped by the work itself.

The Eight of Pentacles reflects this exact stage. The figure is not a master. They are becoming one. Their authority does not come from title or recognition. It comes from contact – from remaining with the work long enough for the work to reshape them.

The Myth of the Craftsperson

In many mythic traditions, the craftsperson held a unique position. They did not command power. They embodied it. Figures such as Hephaestus in Greek myth or Wayland the Smith in Germanic tradition were not rulers. They were makers. Their strength came from what they could produce repeatedly and reliably, and this reliability granted them a form of authority that did not depend on visibility or social position.

The Eight of Pentacles reflects this same mythic logic. Skill is not spectacle. It is continuity made visible.

Repetition as Transformation

Modern culture often treats repetition as monotonous. Myth understood it differently. Repetition was how form entered the body. Each action refined the next. Each attempt adjusted perception. Over time, the person who practiced became fundamentally different from the person who began — not through dramatic change, but through accumulation.

The Eight of Pentacles encodes this transformation. The myth here is not heroic. It is developmental.

The Workshop as Sacred Space

In traditional societies, the workshop was not merely functional. It was initiatory. It was where raw material became usable, and where raw human capacity became reliable. The Eight of Pentacles places its figure in this space deliberately. Identity here is formed through doing, not through declaration. Through participation, not through aspiration.

This reinforces the Pentacles suit's central concern: continuity depends on capability, and capability depends on repetition.

Why the Eight Is Not a Mastery Card

It is important that the figure is still working. Still practicing. Still repeating. The Eight of Pentacles does not depict mastery. It depicts the stage that makes mastery possible. This distinction matters. Mythically, mastery is not granted to those who seek it. It emerges from those who remain. The Eight honors the willingness to continue before outcome is guaranteed.

> *Repetition is how form enters the body.*

Closing the Mythic Layer

The Eight of Pentacles carries the memory of becoming capable — not through talent, not through sudden insight, but through repetition given enough time to take root. Its myth is not about achievement. It is about formation. This is the moment when effort stops being temporary and begins to shape what a person is able to be.

This is where endurance becomes ability.

ARCANA LIBRARY

IX

The Nine of Pentacles

FOUNDATION

The Nine of Pentacles marks a quiet but decisive shift in the suit: the moment when sustained effort begins to hold its own shape. Not as potential. Not as practice. But as condition. This card does not describe achievement in the celebratory sense. It describes the point when something that has been built can now support the life that built it.

When Effort Becomes Environment

Before the Nine, effort is still active. There is learning, adjustment, maintenance, attention that must be consciously applied. With the Nine, something changes. What was once effort becomes structure.

What required constant intention now exists as part of the landscape of a life. The work is no longer held up moment by moment. It is holding.

This does not mean nothing is required. It means continuation is no longer fragile. The structure can bear the weight of inattention without collapsing. Rest becomes possible without loss. It is sufficient, not permanent.

The Difference Between Skill and Sufficiency

The Eight of Pentacles developed skill. The Nine reveals what skill makes possible. Skill allows transformation. Sufficiency allows habitation. The distinction matters. Practice prepares. Sufficiency sustains. The Nine marks the point where effort has matured into livable form — where the conditions of stability are no longer being constructed but inhabited.

The Presence of Enough

The Nine does not depict abundance without limit. It depicts enough — enough resource, enough capability, enough structure, enough distance from urgency — that continuation does not feel immediately threatened.

This does not eliminate vulnerability. It reduces precarity. The difference is subtle but profound. Life at this stage is not free from change. But it is not governed by constant instability. There is room to breathe, to assess, to choose what comes next from a position of relative steadiness rather than reactive need.

> *The work has become the world.*

Autonomy as Condition, Not Assertion

The Nine of Pentacles is often read as a statement of self-sufficiency or independence. In truth, it reflects something quieter. Autonomy here is not declared. It is lived. There is no need to prove capability because capability is already present. There is no need to defend stability because stability is already functioning. What has been built speaks for itself.

This is why the Nine carries such a distinctive stillness. It is the first card in the suit where the central condition is not effort, not strain, not management, and not waiting. It is presence within a structure that works.

The Limits of Sufficiency

The Nine is stable, but it is not final. It represents sufficiency at the level of the individual — a life that can sustain itself through what has been built and practiced. But individual sufficiency, however hard-won, is not the whole of what Pentacles describe. The suit's final concern is not personal stability but continuity that extends beyond a single life. The Nine creates the conditions for that extension without yet achieving it.

The Structural Question of the Nine

The Nine of Pentacles asks: can what has been built sustain a life?

The Ace asked whether something could begin. The Eight asked whether it could be learned. The Nine asks whether it can be lived inside. The answer, here, is yes. Temporarily, and within ongoing change. But reliably enough to inhabit.

A Closing Orientation

The Nine of Pentacles rarely announces itself. It appears as steadiness, as reduced urgency, as the quiet recognition that something built through effort is now building capacity in return. This card does not promise permanence. It confirms that sufficiency has arrived — and that what follows in the suit will test whether what sustains one life can be extended to sustain others.

IMAGERY

Imagery, Enclosure, and the Landscape of Sufficiency

The image of the Nine of Pentacles is quiet, but nothing in it is accidental. It is a moment of inhabitation. Everything that appears here already exists within an established condition. The figure is not building. She is living inside what has been built.

IX *The Nine of Pentacles*

The Enclosed Garden

The most important feature of the image is the enclosure. The figure stands within a vineyard, surrounded by a cultivated barrier of foliage and structure. It is land that has been claimed, worked, and brought into order over time. Enclosure carries a specific meaning in

Pentacles. It indicates that effort has crossed a threshold into stability. What grows here is protected from immediate disruption — not invulnerable, but sheltered. This is land that can now produce reliably because it has been secured. The enclosure marks the difference between survival and sufficiency.

The Vineyard as Time Made Visible

The plants surrounding the figure are heavy with pentacles, integrated directly into the growth itself. They are not being held. They are not being harvested. They are growing. This detail matters. It shows that what exists here is no longer dependent on immediate action. The effort that created this environment happened earlier. What remains now is the continuation of that effort through time. The vineyard makes duration visible — it shows what happens when work has been sustained long enough to become environment.

The Figure at Rest Within Structure

The central figure stands upright, but she is not braced. Her posture is relaxed. She is not defending what surrounds her and she is not managing it moment by moment. She is present within it.

Her clothing is refined but practical — not ceremonial attire but the dress of a life lived within material stability rather than one still seeking it. She is not dressed for labor. She is dressed for habitation. The Nine of Pentacles does not show the work. It shows the condition the work has made possible.

The Falcon: Controlled Power

One of the most significant elements in the image is the falcon perched on the figure's hand. The falcon is hooded — not flying freely, not operating on instinct. But it is not captive in the sense of being imprisoned. It is trained.

This distinction is crucial. The falcon represents power that has been disciplined rather than suppressed. Its presence shows that instinct, force, and agency still exist here, but they are no longer operating unpredictably. They have been brought into relationship with structure. The falcon does not threaten the figure. It rests with her. This reflects a stage where internal and external forces have been integrated rather than eliminated. Control exists, but it is quiet.

The Distant House

In the background, beyond the enclosure, a house is visible. It is small. It does not dominate the scene. It sits at a distance.

This placement matters. The house represents continuity beyond the individual – lineage, inheritance, or long-term stability. But it is not the focus of the card. The focus remains on the individual's relationship to what has been cultivated. The larger system exists, but it has not yet become central. The Nine remains personal. The house reminds us that what has been built can eventually outlast the builder, but that stage has not yet fully arrived.

What Is Absent

There is no urgency in this image. No tools. No visible labor. No threat. No instability. These absences are deliberate. They show that the stage of constant effort has passed. What remains is maintenance through presence rather than intervention. This is stability that no longer requires continuous correction.

Reading the Image Whole

Taken together, the image shows that stability can become environment rather than effort, that what is cultivated over time begins to sustain itself, that power can exist without needing to be exercised, and that sufficiency allows inhabitation, not just survival. This is not abundance without limit. It is stability without immediate threat.

The Nine of Pentacles does not show triumph. It shows sufficiency. The figure is not celebrating what has been built. She is living inside it.

The work has become the world.

TRADITION

Myth, Cultivation, and the Authority of Sufficiency

The Nine of Pentacles belongs to a myth older than wealth. It belongs to the myth of sufficiency. It is the story of a life that has been cultivated carefully enough to sustain itself. The Nine encodes the moment when survival no longer depends on immediate effort, and existence becomes supported by what has already been built. Not guaranteed forever. But stable enough to live within.

The Myth of the Cultivated Self

In premodern societies, stability did not emerge automatically. It was cultivated. Land had to be cleared. Soil had to be worked. Structures had to be built slowly and maintained consistently. The Nine of Pentacles reflects the stage when this work had matured into something reliable. This myth appears in agrarian traditions across cultures: the orchard keeper who plants trees whose full yield will come years later, the vineyard steward whose harvest depends on care extended across seasons, the household builder whose labor creates conditions a life can inhabit. These figures did not live from moment to moment. They lived within continuity they had helped create. Their authority did not come from ownership alone. It came from cultivation.

Enclosure as Protection, Not Isolation

The walled garden in the Nine reflects a critical mythic transition: the movement from exposure into enclosure. Enclosure did not mean separation for its own sake. It meant protection from instability. In early agricultural societies, enclosure marked the boundary between vulnerability and preservation. What was enclosed could grow without constant threat, could accumulate, could endure.

The Nine reflects this stage precisely. The self has become enclosed within conditions that allow continuation without immediate crisis. It is protection from volatility.

Artemis and the Sovereignty of the Self-Contained Life

One mythic parallel for this card appears in Artemis. Unlike other Olympian figures, Artemis lived outside the structures of marriage, household, and inheritance. She governed her own domain. She did not depend on external authority to define her stability. Her sovereignty was not granted. It was maintained.

This distinction matters. Artemis did not escape material reality. She mastered her relationship to it. The Nine of Pentacles reflects this same condition – stability that exists because it has been cultivated and protected, not bestowed.

The Myth of Earned Environment

The deeper myth encoded here is not about wealth. It is about environment. The Nine describes the moment when a person no longer lives at the mercy of unstable conditions but inside conditions shaped by sustained effort. Survival does not depend entirely on what happens next. It depends on what has already been built.

This is a profound mythic transition. It marks the emergence of the self as a stable unit within material reality. Not invulnerable. But no longer precarious.

Authority Without Urgency

The Nine also encodes a specific kind of authority – not authority over others, but authority over one's own continuation. This authority is quiet. It exists because it has been proven over time. The person who inhabits the Nine has learned how to maintain, how to preserve, and how to live inside what has been created. This authority cannot be granted suddenly. It emerges through duration.

Closing the Mythic Layer

The Nine of Pentacles tells the myth of a life that can now sustain itself. Not effortlessly. Not permanently. But reliably. This is where endurance becomes environment, where effort becomes stability, where survival becomes inhabitation.

The card does not promise permanence. It shows sufficiency – and in doing so, it creates the conditions for the suit's final concern: whether what sustains one life can be extended beyond it.

> *Autonomy here is not declared. It is lived.*

X

The Ten of Pentacles

FOUNDATION

The Ten of Pentacles names the suit's final and most profound shift: the moment when something no longer depends on a single person to continue. Not as effort. Not as skill. Not as something maintained through vigilance. But as something that can remain. This card does not describe achievement. It describes continuity – the point where what has been built becomes capable of outlasting the life that built it.

When Stability Becomes Structure

In the Nine, stability existed within a single life. What had been built could support the person who created it, but it still depended on their presence. The Ten brings something different. What exists now has moved beyond personal maintenance. It has taken on a structure of its own – sustained through systems, relationships, agreements, and shared recognition rather than effort alone. This does not mean it is permanent. It means it is no longer fragile.

The Shift from Self-Reliance to Inheritance

Before the Ten, continuity depends on the individual. Skill must be practiced. Resources must be guarded. Stability must be actively maintained. The Ten marks the point where continuity becomes transferable – where what exists can be shared, inherited, passed forward, or lived inside by others. The emphasis shifts from creation to preservation, from building to belonging.

This is a fundamental reorientation. The earlier cards asked whether something could survive the conditions it encountered. The Ten asks whether it can survive the absence of its maker.

Continuity Without Urgency

Unlike earlier Pentacles cards, the Ten carries no sense of strain. Nothing is being forced into place. Nothing is being held together through effort. What exists now has settled. This often feels quieter than expected – there may be no dramatic moment of arrival, only the gradual recognition that something has become reliable enough to outlast immediate need. It is establishment.

The Presence of Time

The Ten of Pentacles is deeply concerned with time, but not the time of effort or the time of waiting. It is concerned with the time of transmission – the time through which something survives its maker, where continuity no longer depends on constant attention. This does not remove responsibility. It redistributes it. Care becomes shared. Maintenance becomes collective. Existence becomes less precarious.

> *The greatest success was not acquiring more. It was ensuring that what existed would remain.*

Stability Does Not Require Perfection

The Ten does not describe flawless security. Structures can still change. Conditions can still shift. Nothing in the Tarot escapes time entirely. But what exists here has weight. It cannot disappear easily. It has roots. This is what distinguishes the Ten from the Nine. The Nine stands alone. The Ten belongs to something larger.

Choice Within Continuity

The appearance of the Ten does not obligate participation. A person may inherit stability and still choose differently — may remain inside it, may alter it, may leave it. The card does not prescribe loyalty. It describes what exists. Awareness of inherited structure allows relationship with it. It does not demand agreement.

How the Ten Completes the Suit

As the final numbered card in the Pentacles sequence, the Ten answers the question first asked by the Ace: can this remain? The answer, here, is yes. Not because effort never faltered. Not because conditions were easy. But because continuity was built slowly enough to hold. This is the culmination of the Pentacles arc — from availability to balance, from balance to coordination, from coordination to protection, through loss and recovery, through patience and practice and sufficiency, arriving finally at inheritance. Not all beginnings reach this point. This one has.

A Closing Orientation

The Ten of Pentacles rarely announces itself. It appears as structures that did not have to be invented, support that did not have to be earned alone, and conditions that remain even when attention turns elsewhere. The card does not ask for admiration. It asks for recognition — the quiet acknowledgment that something has been carried far enough, by enough hands, over enough time, to hold on its own.

What matters is not how impressive it appears. What matters is that it can continue.

IMAGERY

Imagery, Inheritance, and the Architecture of Continuity

The image of the Ten of Pentacles is unlike any other in the suit. Where earlier cards focused on individuals working, balancing, guarding, or tending, this image shows a complete environment. Nothing here is in the process of being built. Everything already exists. The central subject of the card is not a person. It is a world.

X *The Ten of Pentacles*

The Elder at the Threshold

At the foreground sits an elderly figure, wrapped in patterned robes. He does not stand. He does not act. He remains. This posture is important – his stillness indicates that his role is no longer to build or maintain, but to witness. The intricate designs on his clothing echo the Pentacles themselves, visually linking him to the structure that surrounds him. He is not separate from the system. He is its living memory.

THe occupies the threshold space – not fully inside the household, not fully outside it. This position reflects his function. He represents transmission. Not creation. Not ownership. But continuity across time.

The Child and the Animal

Nearby, a child stands with a dog. Neither appears to be consciously engaging with the elder. This detail is precise. Continuity does not require understanding. The child inherits stability before knowing how it was built. The dog reinforces this instinctual continuity – animals live within structures without needing to interpret them. They trust the environment as given.

Together, the child and dog represent participation without authorship. They belong to what already exists.

The Archway: Boundary Between Worlds

Behind them stands a large stone archway. This is one of the most important features of the card. An archway marks transition – it separates inside from outside, protection from exposure, structure from uncertainty. Unlike the open landscapes of earlier Pentacles cards, this image is enclosed. The arch signals that the work of establishment has already occurred. What exists here has walls, limits, and definition. This is not a place being built. It is a place being inhabited.

The Family Within

Inside the archway, figures converse calmly. They are not laboring. They are not negotiating survival. They are living. This distinction matters. The Ten does not depict the creation of stability. It depicts life inside stability. Their attention is directed toward one another, not toward maintaining the structure itself. The system supports them without constant intervention. Continuity has become environment.

The Pattern of Pentacles

The ten Pentacles are arranged throughout the image. They are not held. They are not earned. They are embedded into the architecture, into the robes, into the walls, into the environment itself. This visual choice reinforces the card's central condition: stability has become structural rather than personal. No single figure controls it. No single figure maintains it. It exists as part of the world.

The Elder's Position Outside the Arch

The elder sits outside the inner enclosure while the others remain inside. This spatial separation is precise. He belongs to the origin of the structure but no longer lives inside its daily function. This reflects the natural progression of continuity – what is built eventually becomes independent of its builder. The creator moves to the threshold. The system continues without them. It is completion, not exile.

The Stillness of the Entire Image

Unlike the movement of the Two or the labor of the Eight, nothing here is in motion. The figures are calm. The animals are calm. The structure is complete. This stillness communicates something essential: nothing needs to be proven, stabilized, or rushed. This is what stability looks like after survival is no longer uncertain.

Reading the Image Whole

Taken together, the image shows continuity existing beyond individual effort, stability functioning as environment rather than task, inheritance preceding understanding, structures outlasting their creators, and belonging replacing survival. The Ten of Pentacles does not depict success. It depicts persistence.

This image is not concerned with achievement. It is concerned with what remains after achievement is no longer the central task. Earlier Pentacles cards asked whether something could survive. This image answers differently. It has survived. Now the question becomes: what happens inside what has survived?

The Ten of Pentacles shows that survival, when sustained long enough, becomes a world. Not something built. Something lived within.

TRADITION

The Myth of the House That Outlives Its Builder

The Ten of Pentacles belongs to one of the oldest myths human beings have ever told: the myth of the house that endures beyond the life of the one who built it. This is not a myth of achievement. It is a myth of continuity. It asks a different question than the earlier Pentacles cards. Not whether something can survive – but what happens when it does.

The House as Sacred Structure

In premodern societies, survival did not belong to individuals. It belonged to houses. A house was not simply a building. It was a continuity of land, name, memory, and obligation. It existed across generations. People were born into it, contributed to it, and eventually died within its protection. The house held land, tools, animals, skills, knowledge, and social standing. The individual did not create this structure alone. They inherited it. And in turn, they were responsible for carrying it forward.

The Ten of Pentacles reflects this cosmology precisely. The stability shown in the card is not personal success. It is inherited survival.

Ancestral Continuity

Many mythic traditions center on the idea that the living exist inside a structure built by the dead. Ancestors were not abstract figures. They were active participants in continuity. Their labor shaped the conditions that allowed future generations to live.

This belief appears across cultures — in Roman household cults, where ancestors were honored as protectors of the home; in Norse ancestral land traditions, where inheritance tied identity to place; and in medieval craft and agricultural systems, where skills and land passed through lineage. The Ten of Pentacles encodes this same structure. What exists in the card was not created in a single lifetime. It was accumulated, maintained, and carried forward.

Wealth as Stability, Not Accumulation

Modern culture often treats wealth as accumulation — something to acquire, increase, and display. The mythic worldview behind the Ten understood wealth differently. Wealth meant continuity. It meant having enough land to grow food, enough tools to work, enough structures to provide shelter, and enough knowledge to maintain all of it. The purpose of wealth was not expansion. It was endurance. The greatest success was not acquiring more. It was ensuring that what existed would remain.

The Elder as Living Ancestor

The elder figure in the card reflects the archetype of the ancestor who has completed their role. They are no longer responsible for building or defending the structure. They have already done that work. Their presence marks the transition from creation to inheritance. They remain as witness.

This figure appears across mythic traditions — the retired king who passes the kingdom to the next generation, the elder craftsperson who no longer works but whose skill remains embedded in the community, the ancestor whose labor becomes invisible because it has already succeeded. Their authority comes not from action, but from endurance.

Stability That No Longer Requires Effort

The Ten represents a rare condition: a structure stable enough to function without constant repair. Earlier Pentacles cards required vigilance, balance, labor, and protection. This card reflects what happens when those efforts succeed long enough. The structure becomes self-sustaining. People live inside it without needing to constantly defend its existence. This is not permanent. But it is real.

The Myth of Participation, Not Ownership

One of the most important truths encoded in the Ten is that no one truly owns what they inherit. They participate in it. They care for it temporarily. They pass it forward. The myth rejects the idea of permanent possession. Everything exists within continuity, and each generation becomes a steward rather than a creator.

This reframes success entirely. Success is not building something for oneself. It is building something that survives.

The Limits of the Myth

The Ten does not promise that continuity will last forever. All structures eventually change. All houses eventually fall. All lineages eventually end. But this does not diminish the myth. Its purpose is not permanence. Its purpose is duration — honoring the reality that something can remain long enough to support life beyond its origin.

Closing the Mythic Layer

The Ten of Pentacles encodes the moment when survival has extended beyond individual effort and become environment. This is the myth of stability carried across generations, the myth of inheritance, the myth of the house that continues after the builder is gone.

It reflects a truth at the heart of the Pentacles suit: matter, when cared for long enough, becomes continuity. Not something held. Something belonged to.

ARCANA LIBRARY

XI

The Page of Pentacles

FOUNDATION

The Page of Pentacles opens a new kind of beginning. Not the arrival of matter, as with the Ace. Not the inheritance of structure, as with the Ten. But the moment when material reality becomes something that can be studied, understood, and learned. This card does not describe possession. It describes attention. The Page stands at the threshold where participation in the material world becomes conscious.

When Attention Turns Toward the Material World

Before the Page appears, a person may live within material conditions without examining them — using resources without understanding their origin, benefiting from structures without knowing how those structures are maintained. The Page marks the moment when this changes. Something in the material world becomes worthy of careful attention. A skill, a discipline, a craft, a field of study — not because it promises immediate reward, but because it reveals depth.

The Page does not yet know how to work with matter reliably. But they have begun to notice that it can be learned. This is a subtle but decisive shift. The numbered cards traced the life cycle of material form from arrival through inheritance. The court cards begin something different: the development of the person who engages with that form.

Curiosity Without Mastery

The Page of Pentacles does not describe expertise. It describes willingness. At this stage, knowledge is incomplete. Skill is undeveloped. Mistakes are inevitable. It is the condition of learning.

The Page is not burdened by responsibility yet. They are not required to produce or sustain. They are allowed to observe, to experiment, to practice without the weight of consequence that later court cards will carry. This is the first appearance in the suit of deliberate relationship with material reality. Not survival. Not inheritance. Study.

Learning as Participation in Reality

The Page represents a shift from receiving stability to understanding how stability is created. This shift is subtle — the Page does not yet carry the weight of sustaining systems. But they have begun to recognize that systems do not maintain themselves. They require knowledge, skill, care, and time.

This recognition is what separates the Page from the earlier cards. The numbered sequence described what happens to matter as it moves through conditions. The Page describes what happens to a person when they begin to pay attention to how matter works. The suit is no longer asking whether something can endure. It is asking whether someone will learn how endurance is achieved.

> *Labor transforms the world. Study transforms the person.*

The Fragility of Early Commitment

At this stage, continuation is not guaranteed. Interest may fade. Practice may stop. Discipline may not yet be strong enough to endure difficulty. This is natural. The Page does not promise mastery. It marks the moment when mastery becomes possible. This fragility is worth acknowledging rather than dismissing. Everything that follows in the court sequence – the Knight's sustained effort, the Queen's cultivated authority, the King's established command – depends on this early willingness to remain. The Page is the root system. Without it, nothing that grows above can hold.

Choice at the Threshold

The Page does not compel continuation. A person may turn away from what they have begun to study, may abandon practice, may return to unconscious participation. The Tarot does not judge this. It simply shows that awareness has appeared, and with it, choice. The material world is no longer something that merely happens. It is something that can be engaged with deliberately.

This is why the Page occupies a threshold rather than a destination. It does not describe what will be learned. It describes the condition in which learning becomes possible — the alignment of attention, willingness, and material reality that precedes all skill.

A Closing Orientation

The Page of Pentacles often appears quietly — as interest, as curiosity, as the desire to understand something that once seemed ordinary. It does not announce the beginning of mastery. It records the moment when the question shifts from what is happening to me to how does this work.

What matters is not how advanced the engagement is. What matters is that attention has turned toward the material world with the intention of understanding it. The Page holds that turning. Everything in the court sequence that follows will depend on whether it is sustained.

IMAGERY

The image of the Page of Pentacles is defined by attention. Nothing is being built. Nothing is being exchanged. Nothing is being defended or inherited. The figure is simply looking. This is the first time in the Pentacles suit that matter is not being carried, balanced, or maintained – but studied. The card depicts the moment when the material world becomes an object of sustained curiosity.

XI *The Page of Pentacles*

The Raised Pentacle

The Page holds the Pentacle at eye level. This is not the way Pentacles are held elsewhere in the suit — not gripped tightly as in the Four, not exchanged as in the Six, not worked upon as in the Eight. The

Pentacle is examined. It is suspended between hand and understanding.

This gesture shows that the Page does not yet use what they hold. They are learning what it is. The raised position matters. The Pentacle has been lifted out of ordinary function and placed into deliberate awareness. This is the beginning of study.

Stillness Without Burden

The Page stands upright, balanced, and relaxed. There is no strain in the body, no urgency, no defensive posture. This is not someone under pressure to perform. This is someone allowed to learn.

The grip is careful but not tense — the Pentacle held securely but gently. This reflects an early stage of relationship, where contact is intentional but not yet automatic. Skill has not yet replaced effort. Attention must still be sustained consciously.

The Field: Land That Can Be Worked

The Page stands within cultivated land. The ground is not wild. It has already been prepared. This detail is significant. The Page does not begin in chaos. They begin within conditions that make learning possible. Someone else has already done the initial work of establishing the field.

This reinforces the Page's position in the suit. They are not inventing matter. They are entering relationship with it. The land shows that learning happens within existing structures, not outside them.

The Distance: Mountains Beyond the Field

In the background, mountains rise at a distance. They represent what has not yet been reached — visible, but far away. The Page does not face them directly. Their attention remains on what is immediately present.

This establishes an important principle: mastery begins with what is near, not with distant ambition. The mountains will remain. There is no need to rush toward them. The Page's work is here.

The Absence of Tools

Unlike the Eight of Pentacles, the Page holds no tools. Nothing is being shaped. Nothing is being altered. This absence clarifies the stage of development. The Page is not yet a craftsperson. They are a student. Tools would imply the ability to act reliably upon matter. The Page has not reached that stage. They are still learning what action would mean.

Clothing: Readiness Without Authority

The Page's clothing is clean, ordered, and deliberate. They are prepared but not armored. They do not wear the heavy garments of labor, nor the refined clothing of sufficiency seen in the Nine. This reflects their position — ready to begin, but not yet having earned authority. Nothing in the image suggests status. Only potential.

The World Is Not Yet Asking Anything

Perhaps the most important feature of this image is what is not happening. The Page is not required to use the Pentacle. No one is demanding productivity. No structure depends on their skill yet. This freedom is temporary, but it is real. This is the last stage in the suit where attention can exist without consequence. Soon, knowledge will be tested by reality. But not yet.

Reading the Image Whole

Taken together, the image shows that matter becomes meaningful when it receives attention, that learning begins with observation before action, that skill requires sustained relationship rather than momentary interest, and that development happens within conditions that already exist. The Page does not yet transform matter. They transform their relationship to it.

The Pentacle is no longer just something that exists. It has become something worth understanding. The figure does not know what they will become. They know only that they have begun to look.

TRADITION

The Page of Pentacles belongs to the oldest and most universal mythic pattern: the apprentice. Not the hero. Not the ruler. Not the master craftsperson. The one who has just begun to learn.

This figure appears in myth across cultures because survival has always depended on the successful transmission of practical knowledge. No one is born knowing how to grow food, shape tools, preserve resources, or maintain shelter. These abilities had to be taught, observed, practiced, and carried forward. The Page of Pentacles encodes the moment when a person becomes willing to enter that transmission. Not through achievement. Through attention.

The Sacred Role of the Learner

In modern culture, learning is often treated as preparation for something more important. In premodern societies, learning was itself a sacred phase. To become an apprentice was to accept transformation — not simply to acquire skill, but to become someone capable of carrying reality. This is why apprenticeship in craft traditions was often formalized through ritual, oath, or initiation. The apprentice did not only gain access to tools. They gained access to responsibility.

The Page of Pentacles represents this entry point: the moment when a person stops relating to the material world as something given and begins relating to it as something that can be understood.

The Indenture and the Oath

Apprenticeship in premodern Europe was not informal. It was contractual. A young person — often as young as twelve — was placed with a master through an indenture, a written agreement that bound the apprentice to the household for a fixed term, commonly seven years. During that time, the apprentice received food, shelter, training, and moral instruction. In return, they surrendered their labor, their movements, and frequently their right to marry, leave the trade, or carry secrets of the craft outside the workshop.

The indenture was sealed with an oath. The apprentice swore to obey, to keep the trade's mysteries, and to honor the lineage they were entering. The master swore to teach and to protect. These oaths were taken seriously — broken indentures could be enforced through guild courts and civil authority.

The Page of Pentacles preserves the gravity of this arrangement. The card does not depict learning as casual exposure. It depicts learning as a binding relationship — one in which the learner has accepted constraint as the precondition of skill. The apprentice's freedom returns later, when mastery is earned. At this stage, that freedom has been deliberately set aside.

The Myth of the Chosen Student

Many mythic figures begin their path not through strength, but through selection. Hephaestus, the Greek smith-god, was cast out of Olympus and raised in isolation before becoming the maker of divine tools. His authority did not come from birthright, but from skill learned through sustained engagement with matter. Wayland the Smith, in Germanic myth, was captured and enslaved, forced to work metal under constraint. His survival and eventual freedom came through mastery of craft. Skill became his protection.

In both stories, power did not begin as power. It began as learning. The Page of Pentacles stands at the earliest point in this pattern — before mastery, before authority, at the moment when knowledge first becomes possible.

Why the Page Is Not Yet a Worker

The Page does not labor. They study. This distinction is essential. Labor transforms the world. Study transforms the person. Before matter can be shaped reliably, the individual must be shaped first. The apprentice phase exists because contact with reality changes those who enter into it.

Not all who begin will continue. Not all who continue will endure long enough to develop mastery. The Page represents willingness, not guarantee. They have entered the threshold. Nothing more. Nothing less.

Knowledge as Inheritance, Not Invention

The Page does not create the Pentacle. They receive it. This reflects an older mythic understanding of knowledge itself. Practical knowledge was rarely invented alone. It was inherited, passed down, and preserved. Each generation entered a world where survival techniques already existed. Their task was not to create reality from nothing. It was to learn how to live within it.

The Page belongs to this lineage. They are not discovering matter. They are learning how to participate in it.

The Myth of Humble Beginnings

Myth often preserves a difficult truth: all mastery begins in humility. The apprentice is not important. They are not yet necessary. Their presence does not determine whether the system continues. This lack of immediate importance protects the learning phase — it allows development without pressure. The Page is allowed to observe before they are required to perform.

This protection is temporary. Eventually, skill will be required. Eventually, responsibility will arrive. But the Page does not yet live there. They live in the beginning.

The Transformation That Has Already Begun

The most important mythic shift in the Page of Pentacles is invisible. Nothing has been built. Nothing has been proven. And yet, everything has changed. The person who holds the Pentacle with attention is no longer the person who lived without that relationship. They have crossed a threshold. They have become someone who notices.

Myth understands this as the true beginning of power. The Page does not yet hold possession or authority. Attention.

> *Matter rewards those*
> *who study it.*

Closing the Mythic Layer

The Page of Pentacles does not promise what will be built. It preserves the moment before building begins — when the material world first becomes something worth understanding rather than merely enduring. This is the myth of the apprentice in its purest form: not yet capable, not yet necessary, but present. Willing. And for the first time, aware that what exists around them can be learned.

The entire court sequence begins here, in the quiet recognition that matter rewards those who study it.

XII

The Knight of Pentacles

FOUNDATION

The Knight of Pentacles is the point in the suit where continuation becomes a lived condition rather than a question. In the earlier cards, effort is often shaped by circumstance – something begins, something must be balanced, something is protected, lost, supported, waited on, practiced. At each stage, the underlying question remains: can this continue? With the Knight, that question is no longer being asked. Continuation is already in motion.

The shift here is not into achievement, but into commitment. What is present in the Knight is not a moment of decision, but the accumulation of decisions already made and sustained over time. The work is no longer new. It is no longer uncertain in its necessity. It has become part of the structure of daily life. This is where effort stops feeling like an event and begins to function as a condition.

From Practice to Continuity

The Knight follows the Eight of Pentacles, where repetition begins to form skill. In the Eight, the focus is still on the act of returning — the deliberate choice to practice, to refine, to remain in contact long enough for ability to develop. The Knight assumes that this has already occurred. Skill is no longer in its earliest formation. It has stabilized enough to be relied upon. The question is no longer whether the work can be done. The question is whether it will continue to be done. This is a quieter threshold than it may first appear. There is no visible marker that distinguishes practice from continuity, no moment when repetition formally becomes responsibility. And yet, something has shifted. What was once returned to intentionally is now carried. Not effortlessly — but with enough integration that it is no longer optional in the way it once was.

The Nature of Sustained Effort

The Knight of Pentacles is often associated with discipline, but this word can be misleading if it suggests force or intensity. The Knight does not sustain effort through pressure. He sustains it through consistency.

This distinction matters. Intensity can produce short-term results. Consistency produces continuity. The Knight belongs to processes that do not respond well to urgency — those that require steady application over time in order to remain viable. This includes forms of work that must be returned to repeatedly without visible reward, responsibilities that cannot be completed once and set aside, and structures that persist only because someone continues to maintain them.

The Knight does not rush these processes, because rushing would undermine them. He remains at the pace they require.

Repetition and Identity

One of the most important transformations encoded in the Knight is the way repetition begins to shape identity. In earlier stages, effort is something that is done. Here, effort becomes something a person is known by — not in a social sense, but in a structural one. The person who returns to the same responsibility over time becomes someone who can be relied upon to do so. This reliability is not declared. It is established through duration.

Time, in this card, is not something that passes around the work. It is something that moves through it. Each repetition reinforces the pattern. Each return stabilizes the relationship between the person and what they carry. Over time, this creates a form of identity that is not based on intention or self-concept, but on demonstrated continuity. The Knight does not become stable by deciding to be stable. He becomes stable by remaining.

> *He does not become stable by deciding to be stable. He becomes stable by remaining.*

The Absence of Urgency

Unlike other Knights in the Tarot, the Knight of Pentacles does not move quickly. In many depictions, the horse stands still. This is not a lack of progress. It is a refusal to introduce unnecessary motion. The work this card describes does not benefit from acceleration.

There are stages in the Pentacles suit where movement is necessary – where adjustment, exchange, or change must occur. The Knight belongs to a different phase, one in which the primary requirement is not movement but continuation. Urgency, in this context, would be destabilizing. It would shift attention away from steady application and toward outcome. The Knight does not orient toward outcome. He orients toward maintenance. This is what allows the work to endure.

Commitment Without Compulsion

Nothing in this card suggests that the figure is trapped or without choice. The work could be abandoned. The responsibility could be relinquished. The Knight remains because continuation is chosen – not once, but through ongoing agreement with the work, renewed through action each time the Knight returns. This distinction is essential. Continuation that is forced produces strain, resistance, and eventual collapse. The Knight's continuity is different. It is maintained through repeated affirmation, and this is what gives the card its quiet strength.

A Closing Orientation

The Knight of Pentacles does not describe success in a visible sense. It describes the moment when a person becomes someone who can carry something over time – not because it is exciting, not because it is rewarded, but because it has become part of the structure of a life. The Knight rarely announces himself. He appears in what is already being continued, in what is already being returned to, in what is being sustained not once but repeatedly. And in that continuation, something becomes reliable – stable enough to be trusted, and therefore stable enough to become the foundation on which the suit's final stages are built.

IMAGERY

The Still Rider and the Structure of Continuity

The image of the Knight of Pentacles is often misread because it appears uneventful. A mounted figure sits upon a horse, holding a Pentacle. The landscape is open, the field before him already worked. There is no visible action, no dramatic motion, no sign of urgency. And yet, this stillness is the defining feature of the card.

XII *The Knight of Pentacles*

The Horse That Does Not Move

Unlike the other Knights of the Tarot, who are depicted in motion — charging forward, advancing, or pursuing — the Knight of Pentacles does not move. The horse stands grounded beneath him, its posture calm and steady. It is control, not hesitation. A horse is an animal built for movement. To remain still requires training, not incapacity. The stillness of both rider and horse indicates that movement is available, but not required. Action is not being avoided. It is being governed.

This distinction reveals the structure of the card. The Knight of Pentacles does not act in response to impulse or external pressure. He acts in accordance with what the work requires. Where other Knights embody momentum, this one embodies restraint.

The Pentacle as Responsibility

The Pentacle itself is held upright in the Knight's hand, balanced rather than gripped. It is not being examined, as it was in the Page. It is not being worked upon, as it was in the Eight. It is being carried.

This gesture marks a significant transition in the suit. The Pentacle has moved from object of study into object of responsibility. The Knight is no longer learning what it is or how to shape it. He is ensuring that it remains.

The Red Reins and the Markers of Office

The Knight's armor is muted – the steel blues and grays of practical equipment. Against this muted ground, certain elements appear in saturated red: the gauntlets that hold the Pentacle, the sash crossing the breastplate, the harness binding the horse, the reins themselves.

Red, in medieval heraldry, was the color of office. It marked the holder of authority within an estate or manor – the liveryman, the steward, the magistrate. Red livery was issued by the lord and worn by those who acted on his behalf. To wear red in this context was not to claim personal status but to signal that one was carrying responsibility on behalf of something larger.

The Knight's reds are precisely placed. They appear at the points of contact: hands, harness, reins. The places where his authority is exercised in practice. The places where his decisions touch the system he maintains. His armor protects his person, but his red livery names his function. He is not a freelance adventurer wearing whatever he found on the road. He is a figure whose visible markers identify him as someone the manor's tenants and dependents would recognize on sight.

The horse is bridled in the same red. This is not coincidence. The horse, too, is in service. Its harness is the visible sign that even the animal's strength has been organized into the manor's purposes.

The Plowed Field

The field before him reinforces this condition. The land has already been plowed. Long, parallel rows stretch across the ground, indicating that work has been done and is ongoing. It is the continuation of labor. Plowed land does not sustain itself. If left unattended, it returns to disorder. The Knight's presence in this landscape is not symbolic of preparation, but of maintenance. He stands within a system that has already been set in motion and now depends on sustained attention in order to remain viable.

The absence of visible growth in the field is also important. Unlike the Nine of Pentacles, where abundance is evident, the Knight's environment appears relatively barren. There is no harvest yet, no sign of immediate reward. This clarifies the temporal position of the card. The Knight belongs to the phase of effort that precedes visible result. The work is necessary, but its outcome is not yet apparent. The value of what is being done cannot be measured in the present moment.

The Tree and the Unworked Edge

The horizon line carries two details that are easy to miss. On the right, beyond the plowed field, a single tree stands at the far edge of the cultivated land. On the left, a small green hill rises from a strip of unworked ground.

Both mark the edge of the manor.

Premodern agricultural land did not extend infinitely. It was bounded – by forest, by fallow, by the limits of what one community could maintain. The tree at the horizon is not a stylistic flourish. It is the visible marker of where the worked land ends. Beyond it lies what the manor does not control: woodland, unworked common, the territory of someone else's holding or no one's at all.

The Knight's gaze extends toward this boundary. He is not surveying his own field with pride. He is looking at where his responsibility ends – and where, beyond it, conditions exist that he cannot manage.

This is the precise nature of his stewardship. He is responsible for what is inside the line. He is not responsible for what lies beyond it. Knowing the difference is a part of his office. The work of the manor depends on the discipline of working only what can be worked, and leaving the unworked edge alone.

Armor as Endurance

Even the Knight's armor reflects this orientation. He is protected, but not engaged in battle. The armor is not a sign of conflict. It is a sign of endurance – it allows him to remain in position over time, to withstand exposure, fatigue, and the slow demands of sustained effort. His gaze extends outward, beyond the immediate field. He is aware of the larger context in which his work exists, not absorbed in a single task, nor distracted by distant possibilities. His attention is distributed across time, holding both the present requirement and the ongoing structure it supports.

Reading the Image Whole

Taken together, these elements form a coherent image of continuity. Nothing in the card is beginning. Nothing is ending. Everything is being carried forward. The Knight of Pentacles does not depict progress in the sense of movement toward a goal. It depicts the conditions under which progress remains possible at all.

TRADITION

Stewardship, Obligation, and the Authority of the One Who Remains

The Knight of Pentacles belongs to a mythic tradition that is often obscured by modern readings of the Tarot. In contemporary imagination, the knight is frequently understood as a figure of adventure – mobile, independent, and driven by personal quest. Historically, the opposite is true.

The Knight as Obligation

The knight was a figure defined by obligation. Within feudal and agrarian societies, knighthood was not a symbol of autonomy, but of embeddedness within a system of land, labor, and continuity. A knight was granted land not for personal freedom, but in exchange for service. His role was to maintain what had already been established.

This historical context is essential. The card does not encode the myth of heroic ascent. It encodes the myth of sustained responsibility within material reality. The Pentacle held by the Knight is not simply a token of wealth. It represents the material base upon which life depends: land, yield, provision, and the systems that support them. To hold it is to be entrusted with continuity. The Knight's role is not to acquire this resource. It is to ensure that it remains viable.

The Manor and the Demesne

In medieval Europe, the knight's land was not simply granted property. It was the demesne – land held in direct service to a lord, typically a portion of a larger manorial estate. The knight did not own this land freely. He held it under conditions that required ongoing performance: military service when called, judicial duties at the local court, the maintenance of mills and bridges, the collection and accounting of harvests, and the protection of the peasants whose labor produced the manor's yield. This system bound the knight to a calendar that was not his own. Spring required oversight of plowing. Autumn required the gathering of dues. Winter required judgment of disputes that had accumulated through the year. The land's rhythms set the knight's schedule, not the other way around. To leave the manor for long was to risk neglect that could damage everything that depended on attentive presence.

The Knight of Pentacles encodes this binding. His stillness is not idleness. It is positional. He stands where standing is required – because the demesne does not maintain itself.

The Myth of the Steward

This places the Knight within a broader mythic pattern: the steward. The steward is not the originator of the system, nor its ultimate beneficiary. He is the one who maintains it across time. His authority does not come from ownership, but from reliability. He is trusted not because of what he intends, but because of what he has demonstrated he will continue to do.

This form of authority is fundamentally different from that of the hero. The hero transforms through decisive action. The steward transforms through repetition.

Fidelity to Land and Cycle

In many premodern cosmologies, particularly those rooted in agriculture, continuity depended on fidelity to land and cycle. Fields had to be worked in season. Soil had to be preserved. Resources had to be managed carefully enough that they could endure. Failure to maintain these rhythms was not merely inefficient. It was destabilizing. The system itself could collapse if continuity was not upheld.

The Knight of Pentacles belongs to this cosmology. He represents the human role within systems that cannot sustain themselves without ongoing participation.

The Reeve and the Bailiff

Below the knight in the manorial hierarchy stood the reeve — a peasant elected by his fellow tenants to oversee daily agricultural work — and the bailiff, the lord's appointed administrator. Together with the knight, these figures formed the chain through which continuity was actually maintained. The knight did not work the land himself, but the system depended on his oversight of those who did. Without his judgment about what could be planted, what stored, what released for sale, the manor would fail. This is the historical reality the Knight of Pentacles preserves. The figure on the card is not a romantic adventurer. He is a manager of yield, an enforcer of seasonal law, the visible top of an administrative apparatus that fed entire communities. His authority was practical because the cost of his failure was hunger.

The card carries this weight whether or not modern readers recognize it. The Knight's slowness is the slowness of someone whose decisions affect harvests. He cannot afford to move quickly because the system he oversees does not reward speed.

> *The hero transforms through decisive action. The steward transforms through repetition.*

Duration as Initiation

This is why the card is so closely tied to time. Not time as something that passes, but time as something that accumulates through repeated action. The Knight is initiated not through a single event, but through duration. Each act of continuation reinforces his capacity to continue. Over time, this produces a shift in identity. The Knight is no longer someone who performs tasks. He becomes someone who can be relied upon to perform them. This reliability is not declared. It is established through consistency.

In mythic terms, this marks a significant threshold. The individual has become trustworthy within material reality.

The Covenant of Continuity

The myth does not ignore the cost of this position. To remain is to relinquish constant novelty, to accept repetition, to tolerate periods where nothing appears to change, and to continue without the reinforcement of immediate reward. This path is not driven by inspiration. It is sustained by agreement. The Knight continues not because he is compelled, but because he has entered into relationship with something that requires his continuation. This relationship can be understood as covenant — not in a religious sense, but in a structural one. The Knight's presence allows the system to persist. In return, the system provides the conditions within which his life can continue. This mutual dependence defines the mythic core of the card.

Closing the Mythic Layer

The Knight of Pentacles does not promise recognition. It does not dramatize transformation. It reflects something quieter and more enduring: the moment when a person becomes capable of carrying continuity forward over time.

XIII

The Queen of Pentacles

FOUNDATION

The Queen of Pentacles inhabits the moment when stability becomes embodied. Up to this point, the cards have concerned themselves with the question of continuation. Something appears, is carried, is structured, is protected, is strained, is supported, is waited on, is practiced, and is sustained through effort. Each stage asks, in its own way, whether material life can be maintained under changing conditions. With the Queen, that question no longer organizes the card. Continuation is no longer uncertain. It has become internal.

This is not the beginning of stability, nor the effort required to maintain it. It is the stage at which stability has matured into something that can be lived within – something that no longer depends entirely on active management in order to remain.

From Continuity as Action to Continuity as Condition

In the Knight of Pentacles, continuity depends on ongoing action. The work continues because someone continues to perform it. Stability is maintained through repetition, and its reliability is directly tied to the consistency of that effort. The Queen represents a different stage. Here, continuity has been carried long enough that it no longer needs to be enforced in the same way. The work has not disappeared, but it has changed its expression. What once required constant attention has become structured enough to hold. This does not mean that effort is no longer required. It means that effort is no longer the primary mechanism of stability. Stability has become a condition – present in the way things are organized, in the way resources are managed, and in the way the person within the system relates to what they are responsible for.

The Internalization of Material Knowledge

One of the defining features of the Queen of Pentacles is that knowledge has become embodied. In earlier stages of the suit, material reality must be learned, practiced, and repeated. There is a visible relationship between effort and outcome. Skill develops through time, and reliability emerges through sustained contact. In the Queen, this process has reached a point of integration.

She no longer approaches material reality as something external that must be worked upon. She understands it from within – knows what things require because she has encountered those requirements repeatedly and has adjusted to them over time. This knowledge is not conceptual. It is practical. It appears in the way she manages resources, the way she responds to change, and the way she maintains proportion. She does not need to calculate each action. Her responses are shaped by accumulated experience.

This is why her presence feels stable. Not because nothing changes, but because she knows how to meet what changes.

Sufficiency as Lived Experience

The Queen of Pentacles is often associated with abundance, but this term can obscure what the card actually describes. The Queen does not represent excess. She represents sufficiency — the condition in which what is present is enough to sustain life without immediate threat of collapse. Sufficiency allows space. It allows continuity. It allows life to be lived rather than constantly secured. The Queen is not oriented toward accumulation. She is oriented toward proportion. She knows when something is sufficient, and she organizes her relationship to material reality around that knowledge. This creates a different experience of stability — not one based on control or prediction, but one based on the capacity to maintain what exists without exhausting it.

The Capacity to Support Life

At this stage of the suit, a new question begins to emerge. Earlier, the focus was on whether something could be sustained at all. With the Queen, the focus shifts toward whether what exists can support life beyond the act of maintaining it. The Queen represents the moment when this becomes possible. The system she inhabits does not collapse if she pauses. It does not require constant intervention in order to remain viable.

This is where the card's association with nurture becomes meaningful, though it must be understood precisely. Nurture, in this context, is not emotional expression. It is the ability to provide conditions under which something else can continue. The Queen supports life not by giving endlessly, but by maintaining the structures that allow life to be sustained.

Stability Without Rigidity

One of the risks of earlier Pentacles stages, particularly the Four, is that stability can become rigid. In an effort to prevent loss, systems may become closed, inflexible, or overly controlled. The Queen represents a resolution of this tension.

Her stability is not rigid because it is not based on restriction alone. It is based on relationship. She understands when to hold and when to allow movement. She maintains boundaries, but those boundaries are responsive rather than fixed. This flexibility is not instability. It is maturity. The Queen's system can adapt without collapsing because it has been built with enough depth and understanding to accommodate change.

> *She is not separate from*
> *the world she sustains.*
> *She is continuous with it.*

A Closing Orientation

The Queen of Pentacles does not describe the creation of stability. She describes the experience of living within it — the stage at which continuity has been carried long enough to become embodied, where knowledge has been practiced long enough to become instinct, and where sufficiency has been established long enough to allow care for something beyond mere survival.

The Queen rarely announces herself. She appears in what continues quietly and reliably, in what has been learned well enough to sustain itself, and in the capacity to maintain without exhaustion. Where the Knight demonstrated that continuation is possible through effort, the Queen demonstrates that effort can mature into something that no longer requires constant proving. What follows in the suit will test whether this stability can be extended beyond the individual and organized into form that persists across time.

IMAGERY

The image of the Queen of Pentacles is immediately distinct from the figures that precede her in the suit. Where earlier cards show effort in motion – balancing, working, enduring, repeating – the Queen is seated. The work has not disappeared, but its expression has changed. Nothing in the image suggests strain.

XIII *The Queen of Pentacles*

The Throne as Living Structure

The Queen sits upon a throne that appears almost grown rather than constructed. It is carved with forms of fruit, vegetation, and living pattern, as though the boundary between structure and life has softened. This is not a seat imposed upon the land. It is something that has emerged from sustained relationship with it. The Queen does not stand apart from the material world she governs. She is continuous with it.

The Flowering Robe

The Queen's robe is patterned with growing things – flowers, leaves, fruit. Her clothing does not separate her from the natural world but extends it. Where earlier figures wore practical garments suited to their work – the Knight's armor, the Eight's apron, the Page's plain tunic – the Queen wears a garment that participates in the same logic of cultivation that surrounds her.

This visual continuity matters. The Queen is not dressed for labor or display. She is dressed in a way that makes her body visually inseparable from the environment she sustains. Her authority is embodied rather than declared. Nothing about her clothing announces her position. The position is what she has become.

The Pentacle at Rest

The Pentacle rests in her lap, held securely but without tension. Unlike the Page, she does not study it. Unlike the Knight, she does not carry it outward. Unlike the Eight, she does not work upon it. The Pentacle has come to rest with her. This posture reflects a profound shift in the suit. The material is no longer something to be acquired, balanced, or shaped. It is something that can be held in stability.

The Queen's gaze is directed downward toward the Pentacle, but this is not the focused attention of learning or correction. It is recognition. She knows what she holds. There is no uncertainty in the relationship.

The Measured Landscape

Around her, the landscape is neither barren nor overly abundant. It is alive in a measured way. Vegetation is present, but not excessive. The environment reflects continuity rather than display. What exists here has been sustained long enough to remain, but it has not been pushed beyond its natural proportion.

The landscape behind her extends outward, but she does not turn toward it. Her attention remains with what is immediate. This does not indicate limitation. It indicates discernment. The Queen is not oriented toward expansion for its own sake. She is oriented toward what can be maintained in right proportion.

The Goat at the Throne

Carved into the Queen's throne, just above her head, is the head of a goat. The goat is the traditional symbol of Capricorn — the astrological sign associated with Saturn, with discipline, and with the long, slow building of structure over time.

Its presence in the throne's design is not decorative. It is genealogical. The Queen's stability did not arrive suddenly. It was built by the patient, disciplined work that the Capricornian symbol names. The throne itself is a record of that lineage. What appears here as ease is the inheritance of long effort. The Queen sits where she sits because the discipline encoded in her throne came first.

The Rabbit

At her feet, a small rabbit appears. This detail is often overlooked, but it carries significant weight. The rabbit represents life that continues on its own — a creature associated with fertility, responsiveness, and the natural proliferation of living systems. Its presence indicates that what the Queen has cultivated does not depend entirely on her direct action. Life is now occurring within the structure she maintains.

This marks a critical threshold. The Queen is no longer the sole agent of continuity. She has created conditions under which continuity can begin to sustain itself.

Reading the Image Whole

Her stillness is not the stillness of the Knight, who remains in order to continue. It is the stillness of someone who has become a stable point within the system itself. The throne, the Pentacle, the surrounding life — all of it is organized around her presence. The Queen of Pentacles does not depict the management of material reality. It depicts a body that has become capable of sustaining it.

TRADITION

The Queen of Pentacles belongs to a mythic structure that predates individual authorship. She is not a figure of acquisition or control. She is a figure of environment – one who has become inseparable from the conditions that allow life to continue.

The Keeper of the Threshold

In premodern cosmologies, particularly those grounded in land-based survival, there exists a recurring archetype: the one who tends the threshold between human life and material continuity. This figure appears in many forms – the keeper of the household, the steward of the hearth, the one who ensures that resources are not only preserved, but made usable. The Queen of Pentacles stands within this lineage.

Her authority is not derived from dominance or expansion. It arises from sustained relationship with material reality. She understands what things require because she has remained in contact with them long enough to learn their nature. This is why her power is rarely dramatized. The myth of the Queen is not a myth of transformation through crisis. It is a myth of transformation through familiarity.

The Generative Steward

Unlike the Knight, whose role is to maintain continuity through effort, the Queen represents the stage at which continuity has become internalized. She no longer holds the system together through constant action. She participates in a system that now stabilizes through her presence.

This distinction reflects a deeper mythic truth. In early stages of development, survival depends on effort. Later, it depends on structure. In its most mature form, it depends on relationship. The Queen embodies this relational stage. She does not impose order upon the material world. She works with its existing rhythms, allowing continuity to emerge through alignment rather than force.

The Mistress of the Stillroom

The Queen's archetype draws from a specific historical figure: the mistress of a great household, who governed not through public authority but through systems of provision that determined whether the household survived the winter.

Her work was extensive and unsentimental. She managed the dairy, the brewhouse, the bakery, the kitchen garden, and the stillroom – the chamber where herbal medicines, preserves, distilled waters, and household remedies were prepared and stored. She kept the keys to the storerooms, conducted inventories, knew which barrels of salt pork would last and which were turning, knew which servants could be trusted with which tasks, knew when to slaughter livestock and when to delay. Her authority was rarely written into law. It was structural. The household functioned because she had organized it to function, and any disruption of her systems – through illness, displacement, or death – created immediate material crisis. Recipe books, account books, and household manuals from this era survive in great numbers because this knowledge was deliberately preserved and passed down. The Queen of Pentacles inherits the weight of those books.

The vegetation that surrounds her in the card is not decorative. It is the visible edge of a vast invisible system she has organized into reliable yield.

Care as Accurate Meeting

The Queen is often associated with care, though this term must be understood precisely. Care, in this context, is not sentiment. It is the accurate meeting of material need – the ability to recognize what is required and to respond without excess or neglect. Her discernment is grounded in experience. She does not need to test or experiment in the way the Page does, nor to repeat in the way the Eight does. She knows. This knowledge is not abstract. It is embodied.

> *Care is not sentiment. It is the accurate meeting of material need.*

The Authority of Sufficiency

The Queen is not concerned with accumulation. Accumulation without proportion leads to instability. She governs sufficiency – knowing what is enough, what must be protected, and what can be allowed to grow. Her authority lies in this discernment.

In many traditions, figures like the Queen were not recognized as rulers, but as essential. The visible structures of society – land, wealth, lineage – depended on invisible forms of continuity maintained through daily interaction with material life.

Closing the Mythic Layer

The Queen of Pentacles represents the invisible structure through which systems remain livable. She is the one through whom material reality can continue without distortion. What she sustains is no longer dependent on her alone, but it still requires her participation. She stands within the system, not outside it.

She is not separate from the world she sustains. She is continuous with it.

ARCANA LIBRARY

XIV

The King of Pentacles

FOUNDATION

The King of Pentacles is the final stage of the suit. By this point, the question of continuation has already been answered. Something has come into form, been carried, structured, preserved, strained, supported, waited on, practiced, sustained, and embodied. Each stage has contributed to a single outcome: the possibility that material life can not only continue, but stabilize. The King represents what happens when that stability extends beyond the individual.

This is not the moment of creation, nor the effort required to maintain it, nor even the lived experience of sufficiency. It is the stage at which stability becomes structure – something that can persist, organize, and support life independently of the person who established it.

From Lived Stability to Structural Continuity

In the Queen of Pentacles, stability is embodied. It exists in the person — in their knowledge, their relationship to material reality, and their ability to sustain what is present without constant effort. The system holds because she knows how to live within it. The King represents a further development. Here, stability no longer depends on that embodied presence in the same way. It has been organized into form — into systems, agreements, and structures that can continue even when the original source of stability is no longer actively maintaining them. This does not mean the individual is absent. It means the system no longer collapses in their absence. The King is not simply stable. He has made stability transferable.

The Organization of Material Reality

The King's authority lies not in possession, but in organization. What has been built is no longer held informally or maintained through direct relationship alone. It has been structured in such a way that it can be relied upon. Resources are not only present; they are arranged. Continuity is not only possible; it is supported by design.

This includes the establishment of systems that regulate how resources are used, agreements that define how continuity is maintained, and structures that allow others to participate in and benefit from what exists. The King does not need to attend to every detail. The system carries those details. This is the difference between managing something and building something that can manage itself.

Continuity Beyond the Individual

One of the defining features of the King is that what exists extends beyond the lifespan, attention, or effort of any one person. This creates a different relationship to time. Earlier in the suit, time is experienced through effort – through repetition, waiting, and endurance. In the King, time becomes something the structure itself can carry. This is what allows continuity to move across generations.

The King's work is not oriented toward immediate outcome. It is oriented toward persistence. What matters is not what can be achieved now, but what can remain. This does not imply permanence. Nothing in the Pentacles suit escapes change. But the King represents the point at which something has enough integrity to endure through it.

Authority as Responsibility for Structure

The King of Pentacles is often interpreted as a figure of wealth or success, but these interpretations can obscure the nature of his authority. His authority is not derived from accumulation. It is derived from responsibility – for the integrity of the system he governs, for maintaining what exists, and for ensuring that it remains viable for those who depend on it. His role is not to extract from the system, but to preserve its capacity to support life.

This is why the King's relationship to material reality is inherently ethical. Not in a moralizing sense, but in a structural one. Poor organization leads to instability. Excess extraction leads to depletion. Neglect leads to collapse. The King must govern in a way that allows continuity to persist.

> *He is not great because he is exceptional. He is exceptional because he has built something that does not require greatness to continue.*

The Limits of Control

Despite the stability the King represents, the card does not suggest total control. The system he has established is durable, but it is not immune to change. Conditions can shift. Resources can fluctuate. External forces can disrupt what has been built. The King's strength lies not in eliminating these variables, but in building something that can withstand them.

This is a crucial distinction. The goal is not to create a system that never changes. It is to create a system that can continue through change.

The Completion of the Pentacles Arc

The King completes the movement of the suit. The Ace opened the possibility of material existence. The numbered cards explored the conditions required to sustain it. The Page began the conscious study of material reality. The Knight committed to its continuation. The Queen embodied its stability. The King establishes that stability in a form that can persist beyond the individual. This is the final answer to the question that has been unfolding since the beginning: can something not only exist, but endure? The King answers: yes — if it is structured well enough to hold.

A Closing Orientation

The King of Pentacles does not announce himself through expansion or display. He appears in what remains – in structures that hold, in systems that continue without constant intervention, in conditions that allow life to persist not just for one person but beyond them.

The suit began with a single Pentacle offered into an open field. It ends here, with that offering transformed into a world. Not a perfect world. Not a permanent one. But one built carefully enough, and maintained long enough, that it can carry life forward into time it will never see.

IMAGERY

The image of the King of Pentacles presents a figure who no longer moves within the world, but sits at its center. Where earlier figures in the suit stand, walk, or work, the King is seated upon a throne that is both constructed and alive. Vines, fruit, and carved forms surround him — not as decoration, but as evidence of continuity that has taken root. The boundary between structure and growth is no longer distinct. What has been built now supports life that continues within it.

XIV *The King of Pentacles*

The Established Environment

This is the first time in the suit that the environment appears fully established. Nothing in the image suggests beginning. Nothing suggests strain. The work that once required effort, adjustment, and repetition has resolved into a system that holds. The King does not need to attend to each part individually because the structure itself maintains coherence.

THis posture reflects this condition. He does not lean forward in effort, nor withdraw in protection. He sits fully within the space, grounded, stable, and unhurried. This is not the stillness of waiting or restraint. It is the stillness of completion.

The Bulls of the Throne

The King's throne is carved with the heads of bulls. Four of them appear — two flanking him at the level of his shoulders, two at the base.

The bull is the traditional symbol of Taurus, the astrological sign associated with the earth element in its most consolidated form. Where the Queen's throne carried the goat of Capricorn — discipline building structure over time — the King's throne carries the bull's earth fully arrived. Taurus is not the work of building. It is the substance that has been built.

The bulls also signal something the King's posture confirms: this is not authority through speed or vision. It is authority through density. The bull does not move quickly. It does not need to. Its weight is its argument. The King's throne announces that the structure beneath him is not negotiable. It has accumulated enough material reality that it now sets the conditions rather than responding to them.

The Pentacle Beyond Attention

The Pentacle rests securely in his hand, but it is no longer the focus of his attention. Unlike the Page, who studies it, or the Queen, who regards it with recognition, the King does not need to look at it directly. His relationship to it has extended beyond immediate awareness. It is integrated into the system he governs.

Around him, symbols of material life are abundant but contained. Vines bear fruit. Stone holds form. Nothing appears excessive or uncontrolled. The image does not present abundance as overflow, but as stability that has been sustained long enough to produce reliably. The King does not represent wealth in the sense of accumulation. He represents an environment in which material resources are organized, replenished, and maintained in proportion.

The Throne as Position

The throne itself is a critical feature of the image. It is elevated, but not isolated. The King is not removed from the system he governs. He is embedded within it, positioned in such a way that he can oversee without needing to intervene constantly. This reflects a shift in the suit. Earlier, continuity depended on direct action. In the Knight, something continues because someone continues to act. In the Queen, stability becomes embodied and lived within. In the King, stability becomes organized into a system that no longer depends on constant presence.

The Distant City

Behind the King, beyond the immediate vegetation of his domain, a walled city is visible in the distance. This detail is easy to overlook, but it is not incidental.

The city marks the reach of what the King's structure sustains. His authority is not confined to the personal landscape immediately around him. The system he governs extends outward into shared, organized human life — into commerce, defense, governance, and the inherited continuities that allow strangers to live alongside one another. The city in the distance indicates that the King's stability is not private. It supports a public.

This is why the King is the final card of the suit. The Queen sustained life around her body. The King sustains a system whose reach extends past the body entirely. What began with a single Pentacle offered into an open field has become a world in which cities can exist.

The Distributed Gaze

The King's gaze extends outward, beyond the immediate space. He is not focused on a single task or object. His attention is distributed across the system as a whole — concerned not with individual actions, but with the integrity of the structure itself. Nothing in the image suggests urgency. Nothing requires immediate correction. The King's authority lies in the fact that the system holds.

Reading the Image Whole

This is the visual language of completion in the Pentacles suit. Not the end of activity, but the establishment of a condition in which activity can occur without threatening continuity. The King of Pentacles does not depict control over material reality. It depicts a world that has been organized well enough to sustain itself.

The King of Pentacles belongs to a mythic structure that is less concerned with the individual than with what persists beyond the individual. Where earlier figures in the suit are defined by their relationship to effort – learning, practicing, maintaining, embodying – the King represents a different threshold. His identity is no longer tied to what he does, but to what remains because of what has been done.

The Founder of Enduring Order

This places him within a long-standing mythic archetype: the founder of enduring order. In historical and mythological traditions, this figure appears not as the conqueror, but as the one who establishes conditions that outlast his own activity. He organizes land, defines systems of exchange, stabilizes resources, and creates structures through which life can continue without constant intervention.

This archetype is not concerned with momentary success. It is concerned with persistence. The King does not seek expansion for its own sake. His role is to ensure that what exists can endure.

The Lawgiver and the Charter

The King's archetype is closely tied to the lawgiver – the figure who establishes the formal rules through which a community can outlast its founder. Hammurabi, codifying Babylonian law into a stone monument that would survive his reign by millennia. Solon, restructuring Athenian debt and citizenship in ways that made later democratic experiments possible. The medieval kings who issued charters defining what cities could govern themselves, what guilds could organize, what lands were held under what terms.

What unites these figures is not personal charisma or military success. It is the act of writing structure into a form that did not require their continued presence to remain in force. A law that needs the lawgiver to enforce it will collapse with him. A law that has been so well-formed that others can apply it across generations becomes the founding fact of a civilization.

The King of Pentacles encodes this distinction. He does not represent the strong man. He represents the one who has written something that no longer needs him.

Authority Through Integration

This requires a different form of authority — one based not on force or charisma, but on structural understanding. The King must know how systems function over time, must recognize the limits of resources, and must understand the consequences of imbalance. This knowledge is not abstract. It is derived from the entire progression of the suit. The King carries within him the lessons of beginning, balancing, preserving, losing, receiving, waiting, practicing, sustaining, and embodying. His authority is the result of integration.

In mythic terms, this makes him distinct from earlier rulers or heroes. The hero transforms through action. The King transforms through accumulation — of knowledge, of experience, of relationship to material reality. He becomes capable of establishing order because he has encountered disorder and learned how it arises.

Stewardship at Scale

The King's authority is inseparable from responsibility. He is responsible not only for maintaining what exists, but for ensuring that it remains viable for those who depend on it. His role is not to extract value, but to preserve the conditions under which value can continue to be generated.

This brings a critical dimension to the myth: stewardship at scale. In earlier stages, stewardship is personal. The Knight maintains through effort. The Queen sustains through relationship. The King extends this stewardship into systems that operate beyond individual capacity. This is the point at which continuity becomes institutional – not in the sense of rigid control, but in the sense of organized persistence.

The Estate and the Entail

The King's relationship to material reality is also expressed in a specific legal institution: the entail. An entailed estate could not be sold, divided, or alienated by any single heir. It passed intact to the next generation, and the next, bound by the founder's original terms. This was not designed to enrich any one person. It was designed to ensure that what had been built could not be dismantled by an individual descendant's poor judgment, debt, or whim. The entail is the legal embodiment of the King's mythic function. He has organized continuity into a form that resists the volatility of any single life. The land remains organized whether the heirs are wise or foolish. The system holds even when the people inside it fail.

This is the strongest possible argument the suit makes for the authority of structure over personality. The King is not great because he is exceptional. He is exceptional because he has built something that does not require greatness to continue.

The entail organizes continuity into form that can be inherited; what is inherited then becomes the conditions of a new arrival, and the cycle continues.

> *He has written something that no longer needs him.*

Durability, Not Permanence

The King does not eliminate change. He builds something that can withstand it. This reflects a broader mythic principle: that true stability is not the absence of change, but the capacity to continue through it. The King embodies this principle. He does not promise permanence. He establishes durability.

In many traditions, figures who occupy this archetypal role are remembered not for what they achieved in a single moment, but for what remained after them. Their legacy is not defined by action, but by structure.

Closing the Mythic Layer

This is the final movement of the Pentacles suit. The question that began with the Ace — whether something can exist — has been answered fully. Not only can it exist, it can endure. Not only can it endure, it can be organized in such a way that it supports life beyond its origin.

The King of Pentacles is not the culmination of effort alone. He is the establishment of a world that holds.

Continuing the Work

The Pentacles volume is one of three parts of the same work. Each part carries the cards in a different way; together they form the program.

THE BOOK

You are reading it. Whether in paperback, ebook, or audiobook, the book carries the first three layers of each card – the structural *Foundation*, the *Imagery* read whole, and the *Tradition* from which the card emerged. This is the doctrine of the suit.

THE MEDITATIONS

Each card has its own recorded meditation, designed to let the card be entered rather than read about. The meditations carry the fourth layer of the program – the layer that cannot be read silently. Available at gristtheology.com/arcana.

THE WORKBOOK

The companion workbook carries the fifth layer – the journaling work, the diagnostic prompts, the structured questions that let each card be worked through in your own life. The book describes what the cards govern; the workbook lets you live with them. Available at gristtheology.com/arcana.

The book gives you the doctrine. The meditations give you the encounter. The workbook gives you the practice. Together, they let the Pentacles be inhabited rather than only understood.

Image Credits

The card images reproduced in this book are from the Rider–Waite–Smith Tarot deck, originally published in 1909.

All cards illustrated by Pamela Colman Smith (1878–1951).

Card images via Wikimedia Commons. Public domain.

The original Rider–Waite–Smith deck has been in the public domain in the United States since 1966. The high-resolution scans used in this volume were made available through Wikimedia Commons under public domain dedication.

About the Author

Kristi Hall is a polytheist theologian, author, and publisher operating under the Grist imprint. Her work develops a theology of matter, time, and authority across a series of libraries: Turn (the Wheel of the Year), Hours, Stone, Arcana, Sphere, Money, and the forthcoming Hue. *Pentacles* is the first volume in the Arcana Library.

Find more at gristtheology.com.

www.ingramcontent.com/pod-product-compliance
Ingram Content Group UK Ltd.
Pitfield, Milton Keynes, MK11 3LW, UK
UKHW021838270726
14058UKWH00002B/220

9 798994 910672